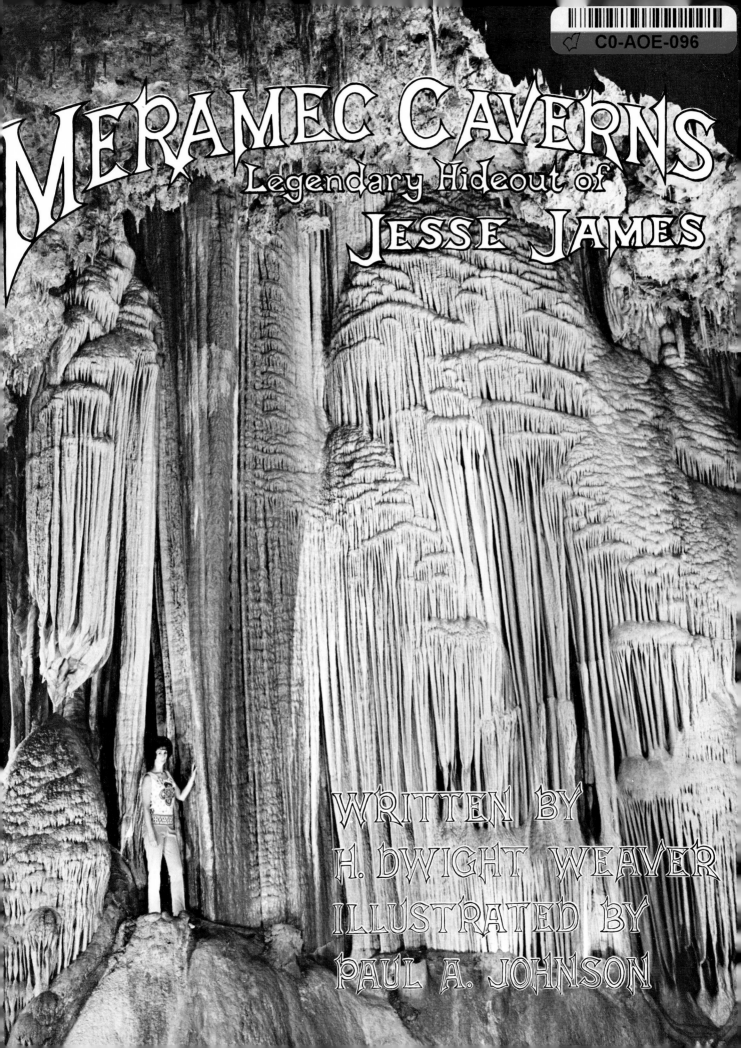

MERAMEC CAVERNS
Legendary Hideout of
JESSE JAMES

WRITTEN BY
H. DWIGHT WEAVER
ILLUSTRATED BY
PAUL A. JOHNSON

COPYRIGHT

AUGUST 1977

BY

H. DWIGHT WEAVER

AND

PAUL A. JOHNSON

FIRST PRINTING AUGUST 1977

A PUBLICATION OF

DISCOVERY ENTERPRISES

2006 DAISY LANE

JEFFERSON CITY, MO 65101

DARK PATHWAY SERIES
BOOK THREE

CONTENTS

ACKNOWLEDGEMENTS

The bibliography and notes indicate my indebtedness to many a person, both writer and non-writer. I am especially indebted to innumerable unidentified journalists who, in the course of their duties, composed news releases which provided many items that have made this book more factual and entertaining.

To certain others I wish to express a special note of gratitude including Eddie Door, John Schmuke, Ida Schmuke, Eddie Miller, Lyman Riley, Betty Pruett, Mary Dill, Francina Turilli, Elmer Gowan, John Sullivan and Robert Shatz.

To Anne Johnson and Rosie Weaver I owe a debt of thanks for their unusual combination of editing skills and creative talents.

Robert (Bob) Hudson was especially helpful and gave not only of his time and recollections but permitted me to use innumerable photographs from his personal collection.

Most important of all, I owe a debt of gratitude to Lester B. Dill. I have had complete freedom in my search for information. I have been able to pursue the project at my own pace--a quest that has consumed a great amount of my free time for more than two years.

Much of this study is a reflection of the lives of a multitude of persons who have given of themselves to the success of Meramec Caverns, be it maintanence man, cook, gift shop clerk, ticket seller or guide. I have quoted them frequently and tried to view the saga of Meramec Caverns through the eyes of those who have known it best.

From personal experience, having been on the staff at Meramec Caverns at one time, I can truly appreciate what this cave has meant to the people who have come to know it intimately. But, it should be evident in the story that follows that without America's Number One Caveman, Lester B. Dill, there would be no Meramec Caverns.

H Dwight Weaver

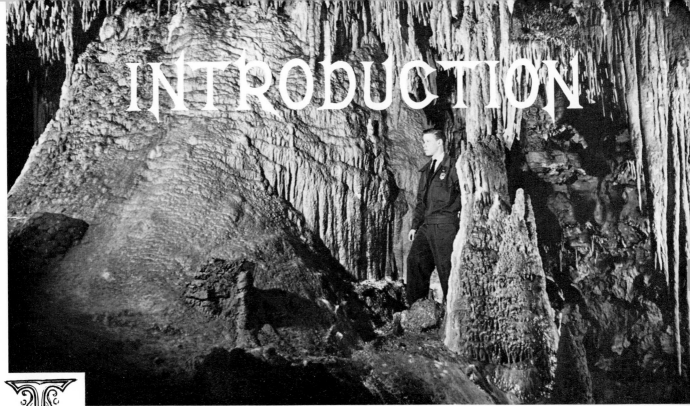

INTRODUCTION

There are more than 160 privately
owned show caves and caverns in the
United States scattered from California to
New Hampshire.* The variety of underground
scenery they present staggers the imagination. For too long their historic sig-
nificance has been overlooked by historians.

Only in recent years has speleohisto-
ry (history of caves) become a recognized
discipline in the study of caves.**Thus
far cave histories have proven to be as
rich and varied as the caverns themselves.

In this study of MERAMEC CAVERNS --
THE LEGENDARY HIDEOUT OF JESSE JAMES, I
was confronted by many pleasant and unex-
pected surprises, not the least of which
is the length and diversity of its past.

Meramec Caverns, known originally as
Salt Peter Cave,+ has a many-layered story
composed of an opulent mixture of fact and
fancy, triumph and tragedy. To uncover
these layers of time we must travel across
more than 250 years of accumulated history.

The first half of this book (Part I)
is a journey through the first 200 years--
from 1720 to 1920. The trail following
from the assigned year of discovery to the
end of the first two centuries was not an
easy route for any historian to trace.
There were many shadows, pitfalls and
thorny problems to overcome.

Fragments of the cave's early history survive in legend and point the way for
our journey. Legends,as opposed to myths,
are believed to have a historical basis
although it may be impossible to fully
document them.

Hernando De Soto is said to have discovered the cave in 1542. The French lead
miner Philipp Renault is also said to have
discovered the cave. The wanderings and
mining activities of Renault in the cave
vicinity in the early 1700's tend to suggest that he may have indeed been the
first white man to actually explore it.

It is believed that Renault established the first saltpetre mines at the
cave. This type of mining activity carried over into the cave's history for more
than a century. A search of the records
of saltpetre mining in the United States
during the 18th and 19th centuries has
provided a basis for reasonable speculation regarding saltpetre mining in
the Valley of the Meramec.

The infamous Jesse Woodson
James is also associated with the
cave in legend and is given some
mention here,but nothing too definitive has been established.
Jesse James is discussed again
in the second half of this
book (Part II).

As we proceed forward
on our journey through
the history of Meramec
Caverns it becomes eas-
ier to determine the
sequence of events
with exactness. The
transition, past
to present, moves
with the events
of that day.

LESTER B. DILL 1976 (Photo by Weaver)

I have made every attempt to not wander too far from the appointed path. If, at times, my assertions seem farfetched on evidence too circumstantial, my only defense would be to side with Bertrand Russell who said "Even when the experts all agree, they may well be mistaken."ϕ There has been an absence of any previous attempt by anyone to seriously trace the sequence of events that form the history of this great cave. There must be a beginning. And I make no claim that this history is without error.

Most readers will find the second half (Part II) of this book more humorous and of greater interest. It deals with the cave's 20th century development as a show cave. The binding element is Lester Benton Dill, a man of truly remarkable foresight.

Lester Dill has been billed as America's most successful caveman, even by his most severe critics.++

He has also been referred to again and again by journalists as "the P.T. Barnum of the cave world."$\phi\phi$ In preparation for this book I devoted some time to reviewing the careers of various show business entrepreneurs of the 19th and 20th centuries to see what justification there might be for the statement. I was especially struck by the comparisons that

could be drawn between Lester Dill, P. T. Barnum, and Harry Houdini. All three achieved high pinnacles of success in show business.

Harry Houdini, the great escape artist, exploited his mastery of human gullibility, for although his feats required great human endurance and skill, he never left anything to chance. In the end, his feats were indeed what they were often said to be--just tricks. $\ddagger$

P. T. Barnum, largely renowned for his traveling circus, exploited the world of animals. For him, prodigies were an object to display. Human oddities were an avenue to riches. Special people, his special success. $\ddagger\ddagger$

Lester Dill has achieved his fame through the exploitation of a natural wonder. But unlike Houdini, who could dream up and create a new escape mechanism, or P.T. Barnum, who could find another oddity, Lester Dill has had to search out ways to promote and sell his singular attraction to successive generations of Americans without the privilege of being able to move his stage to a new location. Dill says "I have to look at it like a moving picture show with only one picture. You keep showing it over and over and pretty soon nobody comes. You have to have something extra to draw people. I've got to keep thinking up ways to get new customers to come in and look at it. I've got to depend on 90 per cent new customers." $\ddagger$

One vital key to the success of all three men has been their total grasp of the nature of publicity stunts. Houdini was especially adept at conveying an idea which differed from the truth but was not an actual lie. He only told part of the truth.

One perceptive journalist wrote that Lester Dill was "a master of the tall tale, and while he doesn't stretch the truth, he is perfectly willing to let anyone who takes him literally, do so." $\ddagger\ddagger$

The personal habits, attitudes and work ethics of Barnum, Houdini and Dill are remarkably similar.

The late P. T. Barnum grew up on a farm. He became a friend of celebrities, was an adroit promoter, and, in the end became moderately wealthy. The same is true of Dill.

Although Barnum has been misquoted as having said "There's a sucker born every minute," his favorite expression actually was "the American people like to be humbugged." Dill has said, regarding his cave visitors "The more hot air you feed them, the better they like it."

To a man, both Dill and Barnum have been described as being cold, emotionless promoters in their relationship with their employees, often creating a climate of opinion that employees are forever subordinate to the success of the show.

Yet, as unkind as this seems to be, both Dill and Barnum are noted for remembering those who have helped them in some way.

People came to admire Barnum rather than resent him. They needed what he had to offer--unusual entertainment. From personal experience I can vouch that the same is true for Lester B. Dill.

From the beginning, Barnum had an amazing ability to obtain publicity. The saga of Meramec Caverns will bear out the fact that Dill possesses the same ability. His life, and the cave's commercial evolution, are reflected almost wholly in uncountable volumes of newsprint.

One of P.T. Barnum's right-hand men for a time early in his career, was a gentleman by the name of Levi Lyman. Levi was known for his practical jokes, great sense of humor, skill as a promoter, and leadership qualities. He eventually left Barnum to embrace Mormonism and served as Brigham Young's right-hand man.

Oddly enough, early in his career, Lester Dill's right-hand man was Lyman Riley. He was gifted with Levi Lyman's same attributes. Lyman Riley eventually left Dill to embrace Mormonism and became an ordained minister and missionary for the Mormon faith.

And, in the final analysis, it seems the greatest achievement of P.T. Barnum's success was the acquisition of a famous elephant.

For Lester B. Dill, it was the acquisition of the infamous Jesse James.

Hannibal, Missouri   H. Dwight Weaver
December 1976

AUTHOR SPEAKS
Missouri Cave Historian H. Dwight Weaver speaks to a group in Meramec Caverns' "Ballroom", Fall 1971. The topic was Missouri Cave history with special emphasis on the early history of Meramec Caverns.
(Courtesy-Meramec Caverns)

7

PART I

THE FIRST
200 YEARS

10

LEGENDS OF GOLD

The forest appeared endless. From the top of a high ridge they could look east or west and see nothing but a sea of undulating tree tops.

To the negro slaves, most of whom had been born and raised on the Spanish-speaking island of St. Domingo, this experience must have been frightening. They were one thousand miles from home, captives in the wilderness, and in bondage to a Frenchman by the name of Philipp Renault. Many did not even speak his language. Any thoughts of escape were probably squelched by the nature of their surroundings.

No one knew what lay beyond the shoreline to the west. Fabled cities of gleaming gold and silver were rumored, but within the almost trackless forests there also lurked wild animals and hostile Indians. Only God knew what else.

Philipp Renault, the son of a noted iron-founder, left France in 1719 with 200 men experienced in mining. He was an agent of the Company of St. Philips and anticipated the establishment of a rich mining industry in the wild unexplored Louisiana Territory.* Near the end of his long journey crossing the Atlantic he had "touched at the island of St. Domingo, and purchased five hundred slaves for working the mines..."**

Renault entered the Mississippi River and "pursued his voyage up that river to New Orleans, which he reached...in the year 1720..."+

After entering the mouth of the huge river they had passed through mile upon mile of marshes and swamps. Mosquito and snake-infested areas were plentiful. And his men recoiled at the presence of menacing alligators that slithered through the murky waters or sunned themselves on river banks far inland on the Mississippi.

Swamps were replaced by backwater areas and moderately higher ground as Renault's long armada of boats approached New Orleans situated on a great curve of the river. The settlement was young, having been established in 1718 by Frenchman Jean Baptiste le Moyne.

Beyond New Orleans the appearance of numerous trees was welcomed. Bend after bend in the wide, sluggish river led them inland until, after many days travel, the southern forests of America began to give way to dense hardwoods. Cottonwood gave way to hickory, gum to beech, willow to elm, and vast stretches of pine, poplar, sycamore and walnut dominated the skyline, Kaskaskia was not far up the river.

Renault "proceeded on his way to Kaskaskia...(and) established himself in the vicinity of this town, near Fort Chartres, at a spot which he named St. Phillips..."++

In 1720, Kaskaskia, Illinois, was just a small village of French traders and their families across

11

the river from Ste. Genevieve, Missouri. It bustled with activity and the presence of this hearty village in the middle of the wilderness was a welcome sight.

Renault established a headquarters in a region now referred to as "Missouri's Old Settlements" territory. From this base he began to plot and organize his exploring trips into the mineral-rich land to the west.

The Old Settlement region is that area west of Ste. Genevieve extending to Potosi, reaching north to Herculaneum, and south some distance below Ironton. Bordering this territory on the west is the Meramec River Valley extending from Salem, downstream to the mouth of the Meramec River near St. Louis. Major tributaries of the Meramec are the Bourbeuse and Big Rivers.

This area was the first cradle of white man's civilization west of the Mississippi. Its mineral wealth has made it one of the greatest mining districts of the world.

Frenchmen made the first lead discoveries in 1701. The arrival of Philipp Renault brought about the tapping of these riches. Mine a la Motte, Mine a Burton, and Old Mines, also known as the Renault Mine, were the first to be opened. From these and subsequent diggings came lead ore, copper, zinc, nickel, cobalt and silver.

Physically, it is a rugged, picturesque land. The highest elevations in Missouri are found here among the St. Francis Mountains. Taum Sauk Mountain, 1772 feet above sea level, is the highest. Deep ravines and canyons, coursed by cool, frothy streams, are found among the jumbled masses of granite rock.

There were but two ways into this wild country in 1720--by river, or by the Osage Indian Trail. The existing forest was so thick it is said that a squirrel could travel from one end of the region to the other without ever touching ground. For overland travel, Indian guides were, at first, a necessity. But the French quickly familiarized themselves with the tributaries of the Meramec River and turned them into highways of commerce.

Renault was encouraged to explore the Meramec River because of earlier reports sent back to France by explorers. Father Gravier, in his journal of a voyage taken down the Mississippi in the year 1700, claimed discovery of the Meramec River, called it the "Miaramigoua"* and stated that a "very rich lead mine"+ was situated some distance up the river. Le Sueur, the same year, also reported the existence of

this mine, giving "the savages" as his source of information.**

In 1542 De Soto, exploring the Ozarks in search of gold, crossed the Mississippi near Memphis but before turning southward, camped and sent two men, Hernando De Silvera and Pedro Moreno and some helpers north to La Saline River for salt.++The La Saline joins the Mississippi just below Ste. Genevieve. Just how far these men penetrated into the wilderness in a westerly direction is unknown but Stevens (1915) suggests they may have been the first to discover lead near modern day Fredericktown.∉

Lester B. Dill believes De Soto or a party of his men may have penetrated further into the Missouri territories than popular records indicate; and that De Soto may well have been the first to see the entrance of Salt Peter Cave. If true, the cave would have been discovered in 1542.

In his march to the Ozarks De Soto had been in search of a rich land called Cayas (Kansas). A tribe of Indians were thought to bear this name and their fabled city to be a storehouse of gold.

Renault was acquainted with the stories told by these earlier adventurers and intrigued with the legend of the lost province of the Cayas. It was said to be someplace up the Meramec River and he was determined to find it.∉∉

For his first expedition, Renault assembled a sizable party of miners and slaves. He also secured several Indian guides.

"They took the Osage Indian Trail" on a course almost due west to where Potosi exists today, inadvertently overlooking the mineral-rich Bonne Terre area. Having crossed the Big River, Renault turned north to a tributary of Big River which he called Mineral Fork.‡

Lead was discovered here. The following year Renault would open a mine at this location (Old Mines) which was not more than 20 miles southeast of the Meramec River Valley and the entrance to Salt Peter Cave (Meramec Caverns). Had Renault continued west across the drainage divide between the two river basins--Meramec and Big River--he might have discovered the cave a few days earlier. But he chose to follow Mineral Fork downstream to the Big River, thence to that river's junction with the Meramec. There were reasons for this. He wanted to search for additional sources of ore along this stream, and to study the stream's course. It was his plan to boat ore downstream to the Mississippi.

INDIAN TRAILS

Countless Indian trails crisscrossed the Missouri wilderness in the 18th Century. Early explorers untilized these existing paths.

INDIAN TERRITORIES

Areas claimed by various Indian tribes before the advent of the Whiteman.

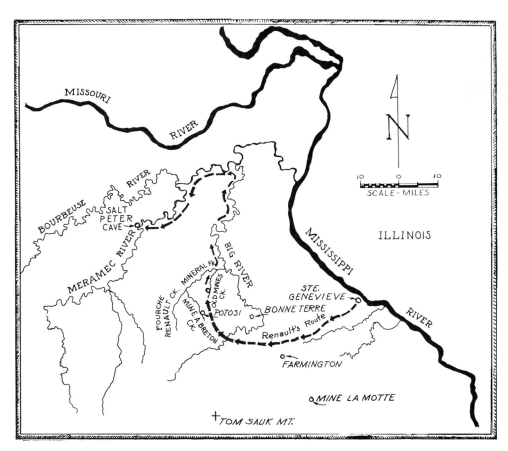

RENAULT'S JOURNEY IN 1720

"This stream from the mines to the Meramec was called "Renault's Fork of the Meramec," and the river up from the mouth of the Mineral Fork was called Grande Riviere. As late as 1800 this river, as far down as House Springs, was called in official documents, "Renault's Fork of the Meramec."**

Upon reaching the Meramec, Renault began following that river upstream, soon reaching areas where the stream meandered along great cliffs and bluffs. The beautiful gray limestone towered up from the water's edge for as much as 100 feet or more and some bluffs swept along the shoreline for miles. For the first time Renault and his men began to notice caves, having probably encountered no others on their trip thus far.

A new kind of excitement rippled through Renault's company. The Indian guides showed heightened interest. According to the Indians, their party was very near a great cave which, to the Indians, was sacred because it was the home of their god "Ucapago."* The walls of this cave, Indian traditions claimed, glittered with veins of the yellow metal so coveted by white man.

Following his Indian guides, Renault was taken to the mouth of an enormous looking cavern. A gargantuan bluff rose above its arched opening. Peering into the cavern itself was like looking into a tunnel to the heart of the earth.

Cold air flowed out past the party of miners. Birds nesting just beneath the entrance overhang cried out, fleeing at the first intrusion. For more than 150 feet not even a torch was needed because the great cavern entrance admitted so much light.

The Indians had no name for this cavern. Renault had given no thought to naming it--but within minutes its name would be born.

The fabled gold veins were, as might be expected, nowhere to be seen in the cool, damp cave walls. Renault was disappointed but peering further than the reach of natural daylight he tried to probe the inky blackness beyond. Obviously the cave continued and the gold might be deeper beneath the mountain. But the Indians would go no further.

Renault queried the savages for more information without results. Some of the miners returned to the entrance to fashion torches for exploration. Momentarily stymied, Renault knelt to examine the soil of the cave floor. He had noted animal scratches at his feet. Now, as he peered close, he saw very minute white crystals

EARLY LEAD MINING

Early lead mining in Washington County under Renault. Painting by O. E. Berninghous. (Courtesy-Missouri State Capitol Museum, J.C.)

14

DRAINAGE PATTERN OF THE MERAMEC RIVER BASIN

had formed in those scratches. Gingerly he gathered some and tasted them. An expression of pleasant surprise crossed his face at their salty-bitter flavor. Saltpetre!

At that moment the big cave acquired its original name, Salt Peter Cave. It was the only name the cavern would have for two hundred years. Eventually, it would achieve worldwide fame for its size,

beauty and history as Meramec Caverns, but this latter name it would not acquire until 1933.

With this discovery by Philipp Renault in 1720 it became the first major cave discovery on the North American Continent and the first large cave to be explored by white man in America. The discovery of saltpetre would bestow additional honors upon the cave.

1765 MAP OF LOUISANA
(Courtesy- Cole County Historical Society)

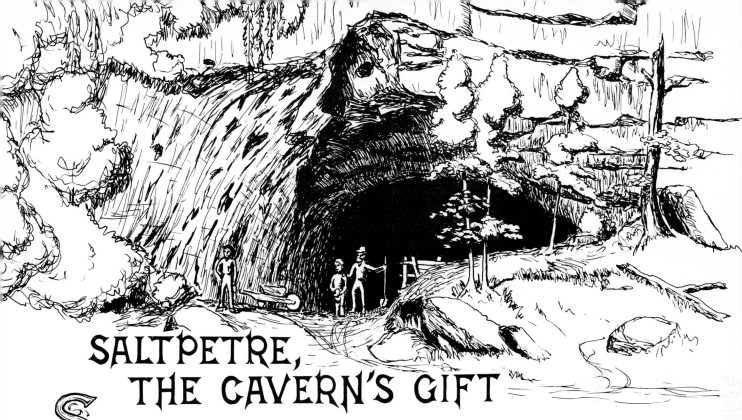

SALTPETRE, THE CAVERN'S GIFT

Saltpetre was an essential commodity of pioneer times. The methods of its manufacture were fairly common knowledge in that day but in modern times it is little known except among those associated with industries producing explosives and fertilizers.

Prior to the Louisiana Purchase, the Missouri territories were inhabited by only a small number of hunters, fur traders, mining adventurers and soldiers. The soldiers were present only because the French government had sent them to garrison the country. They remained until 1762 when Spain acquired the land. Spanish domination existed until 1800. Three years later it became a property of the United States.

The miners, hunters and traders established a few settlements along the Mississippi River, Kaskaskia being the first village. By 1750 more than 1500 Frenchmen were in residence in and about Kaskaskia which spawned such communities as St. Louis, New Madrid, St. Charles and Cape Girardeau.

The Frenchmen, like the American pioneers that came after them, were self-sufficient. They lived off the land, obtaining food, clothing and shelter from the forests, fields and streams. They also manufactured their own gunpowder which required a generous supply of saltpetre. Caves were the best source of nitre (potassium nitrate) supplies from which saltpetre was leached. So, the location and development of this natural resource was high on the list of pioneer priorities.

The search for nitre led to many cave discoveries at a very early date.

Renault brought with him a rather sizable company of laborers and slaves. A large amount of daily supplies were needed to sustain this husky band of outdoorsmen. There was a big demand for meat. This meant large scale hunting, to the chargin of the Indians inhabiting that portion of Missouri. And such hunting demanded a steady and dependable supply of powder and shot.

Aside from company demand, there was also a market for gunpowder among the families of traders and hunters already living in the territory.

Breckenridge (1925) says "It is probably that from the year 1720 when Renault and La Motte opened...the lead mines...they, as well as those who came after them, during the hundred years or more succeeding, made their own gunpowder..."*

Renault did more than just establish the first saltpetre mines west of the Mississippi. It is quite likely he also developed the first large scale saltpetre mines in the United States. Salt Peter Cave therefore achieved a measure of distinction not accorded other American caves. Even though saltpetre caves of the Appalachian Mountain territories are better known as nitre producers of pioneer times, Salt Peter Cave along the Meramec River was the grandfather of them all.

★   ★   ★

The area along the Meramec River, beginning at Moselle in Franklin County and extending as far up the Meramec as Steelville, is one of the richest cave valleys in America. Scores of caves open along the river and its tributaries. Many of these caves are extensive. Some have exceptionally large entrances, and most are accessible to river traffic. Used frequently by the Indians for shelter, these caves supply the river with a portion of its spring-fed water supply. Nitrateous earth deposits are not uncommon in the caves.

More than one chronicler of history has stressed the early use of these caves for saltpetre mining, including Schoolcraft(1819),*Goodspeed(1818),** and Breckenridge(1925).+ Goodspeed in particular states that Salt Peter Cave "is a large opening below Fishers Cave...(and that) gunpowder was made in this cave at an early date."++

From Renault's point of view, the caves would have been considered convenient. First of all, they were located a-

An unidentified cave along
the Meramec River.

long a navigable stream which was a direct route to the Mississippi River and thence to the settlement of Kaskaskia.

These caves were also close to the first lead mines to be opened along Mineral Fork and Big River. The saltpetre mines were dependent upon the lead mines for a supply of sulphur--a by-product of lead mining.

There was yet another convenience-- the existence of Indian trails through the forests. The Osage Indian Trail was a fortunate route between Kaskaskia and Mineral Fork. Other surface mines were opened along the course of the Meramec near St. Clair, Sullivan, Stanton, Bourbon, Steelville and Indian Creek. Two prominent Indian trails existed in this locale, providing a unique system of routes for overland transportation. One Indian trail, which later became a part of the "Freemont Trail" and subsequently the "Springfield Road," followed the ridge west of the Meramec River, then south to Sullivan and Bourbon. Another route passed "near Berryman, Huzzah and Cedar Ford."◊

Renault envisioned both types of transportation--overland and river. He preferred boating ore downstream but knew that this might not always be possible. The overland routes would then be useful for pack animals.

Philipp Renault began work on Mineral Fork in 1721. By 1725 he claimed that he was producing 1500 pounds of lead a day from his collection of mines. The "mines" were surface deposits that demanded no large capitol investment and very little special skill.

Unfortunately, Renault found the stream difficult to use. Even in normal times the rafts, loaded with heavy lead ore, found navigation troublesome on all but the lower 50 to 60 miles of the Meramec River.‡ The Indian trails, particularly the Osage, therefore became the principal highway of commerce between the lead mines and the Mississippi. The lead was transported on pack animals and carts which the Indians later called "barefoot wagons"‡‡ because of their naked metal wheels. Often, the easiest way was to mold the lead in the shape of a horse collar and drape it around the neck of draft animals.◊◊

The constant traffic of heavily loaded carts over these trails transformed them into indelible wilderness roads. Today, portions of these old trails, particularly the Osage, are preserved in the routes of modern highways. The Indians were practical in laying out their trails, taking the topography into account. Their trails usually followed ridges or stream valleys. In the vicinity of Kaskaskia their route was often referred to as the "Three Notched Road"*after the Indian manner of blazing the original trail with three notches in trees along the way.

The number of overseers and slaves lodged in the Meramec Valley for the purpose of recovering saltpetre and manufacturing gunpowder is unknown but it was sufficient to make a considerable quantity of powder.

Caves utilized for nitrate mining lay on either side of Salt Peter Cave. Bat Cave was downstream a short distance, and Copper Hollow Cave, Green's Cave and Fisher's Cave were upstream.** It is presumed that saltpetre recovery systems may have existed at the mouths of several of these caves. The saltpetre, after salvage, was undoubtedly transported to the vicinity of Salt Peter Cave where the largest gunpowder works is generally believed to have existed. This cave's entrance passage was certainly the most accommodating and could

not only house a saltpetre recovery operation and munitions plant, but provide relatively dry, comfortable quarters for scores of men, supplies and beasts of burden.

To reach these caves, sulphur derived from lead mining along Mineral Fork and Fourche a Renault (headwaters portion of Mineral Fork) was taken overland by a convenient route that may have originated on Mineral Fork about three miles southeast of the headwaters of Little Indian Creek. It led northwest (downstream) about 10 miles to the junction of Indian and Little Indian Creeks. Salt Peter Cave and Bat Cave were not more than eight miles due west of this point. By crossing the Meramec River, a connection could be made with an Indian trail (Old Springfield Road) which led along the ridge west of the river to within hailing distance of Bat, Salt Peter, Copper Hollow, Green's and Fisher's Caves. Gunpowder could be returned to the mines and Kaskaskia via the same route.

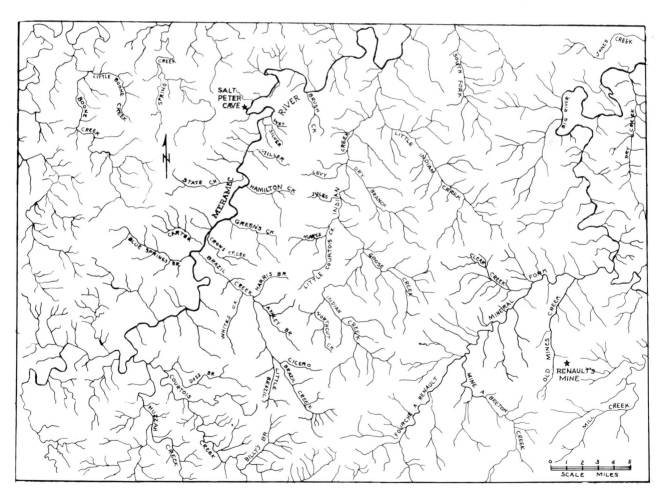

Map showing the complex drainage pattern in the vicinity of Salt Peter Cave and Renault's Mine.

Saltpetre occurs in caves which have alkaline soils, good air circulation, a temperature between 52 and 60 degrees, earthen floors that are relatively dry, and a humidity of between 10 and 30 per cent. Although the chemical nature of the substance is known, the manner in which it originates in cave soils is not yet fully understood. It is thought to be largely bacterial in origin.

Renault and his men identified saltpetre by one of several methods in vogue at that time. Taste was one method. Soils rich in saltpetre contain small, thin, whitish crystals that have a cool, salty-bitter taste. Since Epsom Salts has a similar taste, this was not a definitive method. For verification, the men would scratch the soil lightly and return a few days later to see if the scratch had "smoothed out" and filled itself in through crystallization--a sure sign of saltpetre. Another approach was to gather some of the small white crystals and toss them onto hot coals. If the crystals sparkled and burned, they were saltpetre.

The recovery of saltpetre requires a plentiful supply of fresh water for leaching purposes. Of the five caves known to have been sources of saltpetre at this location and previously listed, only Salt Peter Cave had a spring-fed stream that was adequate in supply and location.

Vats for leaching were box-shaped wooden affairs capable of holding large amounts of petre-dirt. They were so constructed that when water was added, the entire contents of the vat became thoroughly saturated. The saltpetre-enriched water would filter out the bottom into a trough where it stood for several days to permit the material in suspension to settle out. After this, the water in the settling trough was drained off and the residue in its bottom was ready for conversion, a process whereby potash chemicals are used to convert the calcium nitrate to potash nitrate (a very meticulous procedure when done properly). Once this was accomplished the material was ready for purification and crystallization. The crystallization process required that the material be put in kettles and boiled in water to permit the formation of pure saltpetre crystals usable, after drying, for making crude gunpowder.

The making of gunpowder was a hazardous occupation. The crude powder was a volatile mixture. The saltpetre was combined with charcoal and sulphur to make the explosive mixture. When fired, it created great clouds of smoke. Such fireworks impressed the Indians but the flintlock rifles used by the Frenchmen were heavy, awkward weapons of questionable accuracy. The gunpowder was unpredictable.

A hunter was never sure his weapon would discharge properly. He simply took aim, uttered a prayer, fired, and hoped for the best.

★   ★   ★

Both the French and Spanish coveted the Louisiana Territory. By 1719 the Spaniards were quite alarmed with French activities and began launching their own expeditions but with little success. French settlements continued to spring up and thrive along the rivers.

Renault prospered until 1731 when the company with which he was allied went bankrupt and left him to fend for himself financially. By 1742 he had given up and returned to France. The slaves, he sold. Most remained in Missouri territories. The saltpetre mines were abandoned and fell silent. Their great reserves had hardly been touched.

The self-sustaining French settlements continued their existence but had occasional problems with the Indians. The French also became increasingly aware of the influx of British settlers to the east in the Appalachian Mountain areas. Streams of migrants poured into western Pennsylvania. Others chose to settle along the Allegheny and Ohio rivers. By 1760 the

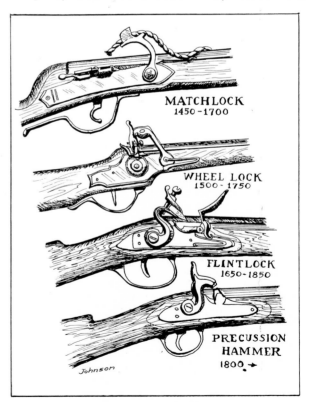

WEAPON MECHANISMS
They all require gunpowder made with sulphur, carbon and saltpeter. Dates are indefinite.

HENRY ROWE SCHOOLCRAFT

Explorer and Indian expert.
He viewed souther Missouri
before Statehood, 1819.
(Courtesy-State Historical
Society of Missouri)

Wilderness Trail carried many emigrants of Scotch-Irish, Dutch-German and English extraction, and Kentucky territories began to see their first permanent residents.

During this period a hard struggle between France and Great Britain existed for control of Canada. It culminated in the French and Indian War which ended with a treaty in 1763. France withdrew from the mainland of North America. Great Britain acquired the eastern half of the great valley of the Mississippi and Spain acquired the western half known as the Louisiana Territory.

Despite the fact that there were numerous villages both east of and along the Mississippi, they were remote and separated by vast stretches of forest. Communication was slow. It was several years be-fore Spain's influence was seriously felt and it was 1770 before the first Spanish governor arrived.

Spanish domination in the Missouri territories from 1763 to 1795 was uneventful except perhaps for the development of the fur trade in the 1780's.

Schoolcraft (1819)+ states that the Spanish showed little interest in most of the French lead mines but they did work the mines on Mineral Fork until 1799. By the same token, they paid little attention to the old saltpetre mines. We know of no organized work at these mines during this period. The saltpetre reserves were activated occasionally, however, by parties of hunters and traders who needed to replenish their supply of gunpowder. The salt-petre mines had become public property.

Legend says that "In 1760, Don Serita Gonzales, with a party of Spanish miners, used the cave for a base of operations for lead mining in Missouri."++ Although the source of this legend is unknown,considering the fact that the Spanish did reactivate mining on Mineral Fork, their possible use of Salt Peter Cave is not unlikely particularly with the presence of the abandoned saltpetre works at its entrance. Their need for gunpowder was as pressing as that of the French, for between 1760 and 1780 there were serious Indian problems.

In 1795 the Spanish government made provision for surveying lands in the Upper Louisiana Territory. Numerous land grants were made along the Missouri River. The nearest land grant to Salt Peter Cave was Land Grant No. 3279 just east of the cave on the opposite side of the river.φ This grant, presumably, was given for the

purpose of mining lead and copper. The remains of an old smelter on the land survived well into the 1900's.

The American Revolution came in 1776 and by 1781 had wrested freedom from Britain for the colonies along the eastern seaboard. During the conflict both France and Spain realized the independence of the United States. After the war Spain realized its inability to defend the Louisiana Territory from American expansion and migration across the Mississippi. In 1800, Spain secretly gave the vast territory back to France. France never took possession and in April 1803 sold it to the United States. It included 827,987 square miles between the Rocky Mountains and the Mississippi, stretching from Canada to the Gulf of Mexico. All of the Missouri territories were now a part of the United States.

Meramec River bluffs near the cave.   (Photo by Johnson)

SETTLERS, SALTPETRE AND SURVIVAL

Under Spanish rule Upper Louisiana was controlled by commandants who governed the region's five districts--St. Charles, St. Louis, Ste. Genevieve, Cape Girardeau and New Madrid. Local magistrates were called syndics and Daniel Boone, who came to Missouri in 1799, served as a syndic for the St. Charles District in 1800.*

No legends are known that associate Daniel Boone with Salt Peter Cave. He is, however, credited with the discovery of Onondaga Spring which is the original entrance to Onondaga Cave located about 20 miles upstream from Salt Peter Cave in Crawford County.** Some families of the Meramec River Valley are believed to be distantly related to Daniel Boone's wife Rebecca Bryan.+ It is said that "Daniel Boone made many hunting trips up the Meramec Valley. He found a beautiful scenic area abounding in wild game of many kinds. There were numerous springs of clear cool water and numerous caverns as well. Boone was entranced with the sylvan beauty of the area and it is reported he recommended that it be made a National park..."++

Daniel Boone arrived at St. Louis in October of 1799 with a company of family and friends. According to the *Sesqui-Centennial History of Franklin County* (1968), Boone "lived for a few years in the southwestern part of the county (Franklin), now known as Boone Township. In 1803 he moved to Warren County..."◊

Stephen Sullivan, founder of the town of Sullivan, Missouri, three miles southeast of Salt Peter Cave, knew Daniel Boone. It was Boone, according to legend, who re-commended the Meramec Valley to him.

Stephen Sullivan was the son of Charles Sullivan of Greenville, South Carolina. Stephen was born in 1795 and "married Dorcas Pinnell when they were quite young, yet in their teens, and went to Kentucky. There they joined some immigrants coming to Missouri. They crossed the Mississippi River at Ste. Genevieve, Missouri, on a boat propelled by horsetread power. They had not been there but a few days when Daniel Boone and two Indians came there from Boone's camp in Horseshoe Bend on Boone's Creek, eight miles west of the present town of Sullivan, to buy ammunition and other supplies. Boone told them of the Meramec River with its clear flowing water, abounding in fish, and the country in game and lead ore.

"When Boone and his Indians returned, Mr. Sullivan and his wife accompanied them to the Meramec River. They found it as Boone had told them and they settled there, where the old Indian trail crossed the river, leading from Boone Creek and the Bourbois country to Potosi. They built a log cabin near what is known as Hamilton Ford."◊◊

The Indian trail spoken of was easily followed in Mr. Sullivan"s time. It was the same trail utilized by the French and Spanish miners in movement to and from the mines on Mineral Fork and the gunpowder works at Salt Peter Cave. The heavy use of the trail left deep ruts in the earth.

In time, the course of Stephen Sullivan's life became a part of the history of Salt Peter Cave, but his initial interests lay in farming and lead mining. With the help of the eight children his wife bore him, and later his acquired slaves, Sullivan cleared a large tract of land which was rich in minerals. He became wealthy, and annually the family journeyed to St. Louis by ox team to lay in supplies of sugar, salt and coffee. They raised everything else.

Osiek and Roblee (1968)* speak of two types of early immigrants to Franklin County--the hunters and the true settlers. The two were incompatable. The hunters viewed the settlers as "too civilized" and the Indians as "too savage." The Indians were soon forced to leave the region for land elsewhere. Eventually, the hunters followed the game and the men of the soil remained as masters of the territory.

During the 16th and 17th centuries the eastern states were populated by two kinds of individuals--those fleeing religious persecution in the Old World, and those interested in the land and its de-

velopment. While people in the New England colonies of the 1700's were embroiled in theological debates and constitutional questions, the territories of Carolina, Tennessee, Pennsylvania, Virginia and Kentucky were being settled by mountain people who were self-sufficient, rugged individualists.

Although these mountain people could provide for themselves well enough, there were two essentials of pioneer life even they found difficult to secure--salt and saltpetre.

Among the mountain people there were many who found lead and copper mining to their liking. With the establishment of each new hamlet came a search for mineral resources in the land thereabouts. Salt and saltpetre reserves were among the things looked for first.

Saltpetre mining was well established in Virginia by the late 1700's, having begun around 1740 at Clark's Saltpeter Cave near Williamsville, Virginia. At least 35 caves in Virginia were mined after this date along the "Old Saltpeter Trail." It began in the vicinity of Luray, Virginia, and threaded along the western border of Virginia south and west for 250 miles to the town of Ewing, just a few miles east of Cumberland Gap.**

Immigrants to Tennessee and Kentucky carried the saltpetre industry westward through the Cumberland Gap. By 1819 the industry, along with settlement, became entrenched in western Kentucky. Ahead lay Missouri as immigration continued westward at a steady pace.

Migrants to Missouri were undoubtedly astonished, upon their arrival in the Meramec River Valley, to discover the crumbling ruins of a saltpetre works at the mouth of Salt Peter Cave.

The very first settlers to Franklin County established themselves near the mouth of Brush Creek about eight miles northeast of Salt Peter Cave, and downstream on the Meramec River. This hamlet, no longer shown on maps, was known as Whitmire (Anaconda). Thoming and Reed (1968)+ report that this group of immigrants originated at Abbyville, South Carolina and "started an exodus westward after getting some followers from North Carolina and the Virginias. They followed Boone's Cumberland Gap Trail and crossed the Mississippi near St. Louis." Among these families were Collins, Apperson, Hearst, Clark, Patton, Phillips, Smith, Enloe, Huff and Williamson.++

At about the same time (1808) William Maupin from Kentucky settled in the Berger-New Haven area in the northwest corner of Franklin County, and was followed soon

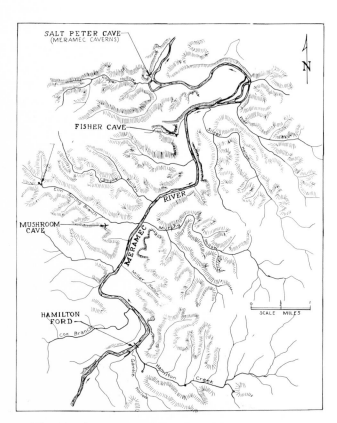

The Hamilton Ford-Salt Peter Cave area..

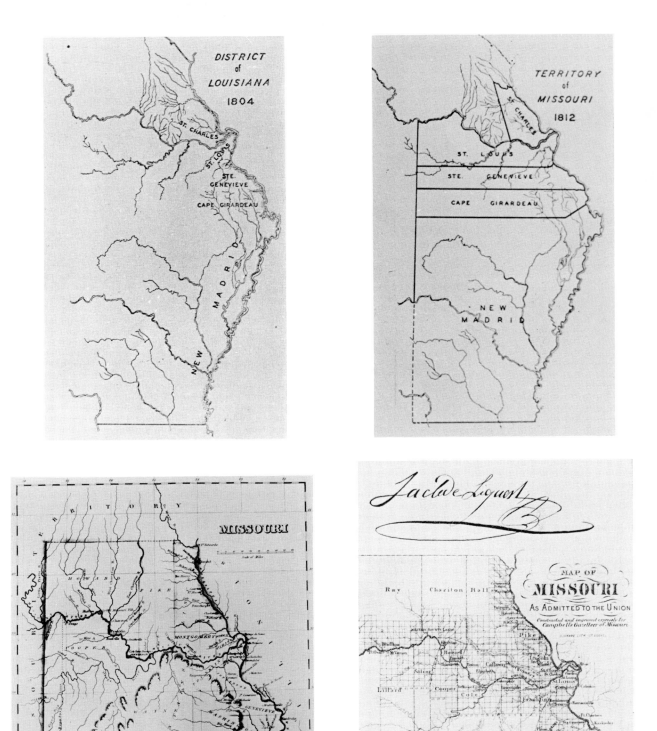

MAPS OF THE EMERGING MISSOURI 1804-1821
(Courtesy-Cole County Historical Society)

thereafter by a William Clark.◊

At a later date (1854) James Campbell from Pennsylvania established himself at Campbellton not far southeast of New Haven and only three miles south of Dundee.◊◊

That saltpetre mining would be revived in Franklin County was inevitable. The Campbells, Pattons, Clarks and Maupins had migrated to Missouri from the east where these same family lines had been traditionally associated with the salt-petre industry.

*   *   *

Hardly before settlement of the Louisiana Purchase began, a succession of expeditions were outfitted for exploration of the far west. Meriwether Lewis and William Clark were dispatched westward in 1805 and followed in the same year by Lt. Zebulon Pike. Both exploration and settlement of the new land began with great enthusiasm.

During the period 1803 to 1812 world events conspired to impede American tranquility and set the stage for the War of 1812 between the United States and Great Britain. Largely fought in the region of the Great Lakes, the action was certainly not as far from the Missouri territories as the new settlers would have liked. However, the conflict did not actually reach them. The only disturbance they felt, outside of bothersome rumors, was increased river traffic and aggitation of the Indians by French and British war mongers.

The War of 1812 did not ignite suddenly. As relations between the United States and Great Britain worsened, a demand for saltpetre was anticipated by military leaders and old saltpetre miners. Along the western frontier where restless Indians began to raid and pillage, the demand for saltpetre skyrocketed. Consequently, the market value shot upwards from 17¢ a pound, to $1.00 a pound--an all time high.‡ It remained at this inflated price until well after the War. In 1816 it was still selling at $1.00 a pound in the St. Louis area.

The heavy demand for gunpowder and the high market value of raw saltpetre, revived saltpetre mining along the Meramec and Missouri River basins within the boundaries of Franklin County. Powder mills sprang up at Molino, Youngs Mill, Spring Creek Mills, Newport, Dundee and Stanton.+

According to the *Missouri Historical Review* "Jack Maupin had a powder mill on the Meramec River in a cave...(and) Fisher's Cave, Saltpeter Cave and Copper Hollow Cave, all...near Sullivan were famous powder making plants from 1810 to 1820."++ Another member of the Maupin family--John "son of Mosias, was killed by the explosion of a powder mill...about Newport."*

By the early 1820's a depressed economy in the saltpetre industry led the enterpreneurs at Salt Peter Cave to give up their efforts and concentrate upon more financially rewarding endeavors. But the cave and its explosive resources would not be forgotten for long. A new conflict would soon be in the making--the War Between the States.

This interesting
Thong Tree is
located in
La Jolla Natural Park.
(Photo by Johnson)

26

CAVES,

AND CANNON THUNDER

Isolated in rugged terrain and insulated by vast forests, the new Missourians had only meager exposure to the War of 1812. The continual stream of migrants to and through the Louisiana Territory brought news from the outside world. But in their remote outposts of civilization, the new Missourians paid little heed to the rumors of war. For them it was difficult enough to hold back the forces of nature, clear land, and try to assure their survival in the new, resource-rich land they inhabited.

In 1846 war broke out between the United States and Mexico but this conflict was far to the south and the Missourians were able to ignore the issue. Yet, in the secluded hills and hollows of Missouri trouble was brewing. In the early 1850's the slave holders of Franklin County probably had little inkling of the price they would pay over the question of slavery. The Abolition Movement and Civil War were drawing close.

Civil War came to Missouri before 1860 as a Missouri-Kansas border war. In the late 1840's the people of northwest Missouri demanded that the fertile lands of Kansas be opened to settlement. A controversy soon arose over whether or not Kansas would become a slave or "free-soil" state. Quarreling between pro-slavery settlers and Abolitionists on the Kansas side created a local civil war. Both factions fought for control of the territorial government. When pro-slavers on the Missouri side began sending reinforcements over into Kansas to back pro-slavery settlers, "free-soilers" then began to raid the Missouri counties on the border. The

Missourians answered with raids into Kansas territory.

Backlash from the border war was reflected in Missouri politics in the election year of 1860 and was sufficient to split the National Democratic Convention. In Missouri, Claiborne F. Jackson won the election on a strongly southern platform.

Missouri tried at the outset of the War Between the States to remain neutral. Governor Jackson was personally in favor of secession but his hands were tied by Union factions.

★   ★   ★

A Constitutional Convention was called to consider Missouri's position and Sterling Price was elected President of the Convention. But a decision seemed impossible.

Meanwhile, Governor Jackson laid plans for the secession of Missouri. He refused to obey Lincoln's call for troops and began arming the State Militia. Strong Federal supporters in St. Louis under the direction of Frank Blair, put arms into the hands of General Nathaniel Lyon and effectively neutralized Jackson's plans. Missouri suddenly found itself virtually without an effective government.

Jackson was forced to flee and General Sterling Price, declaring himself for the southern cause, took up arms for the Confederacy.

The Constitutional Convention reconvened, declared the office of Governor vacant and elected Hamilton R. Gamble as Provisional Governor.

Martial law was established following the ouster of Governor Jackson and by 1862 Federal patrols controlled the major highways and rivers, yet bands of bushwhackers and Confederate sympathizers sometimes controlled entire counties and made matters serious for any Federals that ventured into backwoods areas. The guerrillas brought wholesale destruction to railroads and highway bridges.

Defeat of the Confederates at the Battle of Pea Ridge in Arkansas kept the larger forces of the Confederacy from Missouri but had little influence on guerrilla activity.

Guerrilla activity in the state was so prolific that men like William Quantrill, Bill Wilson, Crabtree, Frank and Jesse James, and Bob and Cole Younger easily created havoc and destruction. They all became infamous for their atrocities, real and legendary.

GOVERNOR HAMILTON R. GAMBLE
(Courtesy- State Historical Society of Missouri)

When Claiborne Jackson began arming Home Guard companies at the outset of the war, much powder and shot was sent to Confederate sympathizers. In some areas of Missouri their supplies were secreted in caves.* After Federal patrols gained control, Union troops began a search for these supplies.

In central Missouri, the Federals hunted Secessionist Capt. William McCubbin and General Crabtree.**Crabtree survived until 1864 largely due to a network of cave hideouts but met his end in August of 1864, gunned down almost by chance.

Along the Little and Big Piney Rivers to the east of General Crabtree's area, Federal patrols fought a losing battle to capture Bill Wilson, a guerrilla of native stock who began his outlaw activities as a personal vendetta against Federal troops that angered isolated communities through harassment, looting and burning.+

Caves were intimate segments in Wilson's escape routes and he was never officially apprehended. He fled the state when the war ended and was not heard from again.

Missouri caves were also utilized, according to legend, as part of the network of the "Underground Railroad" in its attempts to help slaves on their flights

GOVERNOR CLAIBORNE FOX JACKSON
(Courtesy- State Historical Society of Missouri)

to freedom. Salt Peter Cave in Franklin County is said to have been an important link. One undocumented source states that "thousands of slaves found freedom via this route."*

When Missouri entered the Civil War it was a divided border state and it is interesting to note that while Missouri, as a state, had a slave percentage of only nine per cent, Franklin County had a slave population of more than thirteen per cent, this being a carry over from the time of French occupation in the 1700's when slavery was introduced to the territory by Phillip Renault.

The slavery question in Missouri was more academic that real. A majority of slaves in the Cave State were house servants and there were few large plantation owners like those in the Cotton Belt. Only in a few areas of Missouri were there slave difficulties and such problems were short lived.

A number of prominent Franklin County residents were slave owners. The slaves served two purposes, as help in the lead and copper mines, and as household servants. Slaves were a mark of wealth and social standing.

Among the slave holding families of the county were the Sullivans, Campbells, Pattons, Clarks, Maupins and Stantons-- the same families associated with salt-petre mining.

John Stanton settled in Franklin County about 1820 and pursued mining interests. About the year 1855 he and one Peter Stanton opened copper mines about four to five miles north of Salt Peter Cave. In July of 1856 a post office was opened in the vicinity and the community was first listed as Stanton Copper Mines. From this the settlement of Stanton received its name. The town of Stanton, which still has a post office but only a few residents today, was, in the beginning years of the Civil War, the largest population center in Franklin County. This created frequent activity in and about Salt Peter Cave.

Rayburn (1943)**states that prior to the war, Peter Stanton operated a powder mill in the vicinity of Stanton.+ His munitions plant and saltpetre recovery operation is generally believed to have been within the entrance of Salt Peter Cave (Saltpeter Cave). It is said that he simply repaired and added to the existing remnants of earlier operations.

The Stantons utilized negro slaves in their mining enterprises (copper, lead and saltpetre). This associated blacks with the cave and may have later given rise to

rumors that the cave was part of the Underground Railroad.

As the Civil War approached, and with encouragement from representatives of Claiborne Jackson, Peter Stanton increased the output at his munitions plant. The Confederate sympathizers and slave holders of Franklin County began to arm themselves.

Franklin County was politically divided into factions and sub-factions but the majority of the people were pro-Union. Six thousand Franklin County men eventually joined the Union forces. Less than 700 fought for the Confederacy. The large slave holders of the county were clearly outnumbered but they also controlled the wealth. Their position of wealth and social prominence was an advantage at war's beginning but the stronger Union factions overpowered them by 1862.

The village of Stanton was officially established in 1856 and the town of Sullivan in 1858. Saltpeter Cave lay along the Freemont Trail about halfway between the two settlements. War brought a bond of cooperation between the pro-southern Stanton and Sullivan families. Steven Sullivan began to assist in the making of gunpowder at the cave.

A story survives which relates that Stephen Sullivan was executed by the Fed-

General Sterling Price
(Century Magazine- 1887)

29

eral troops because he manufactured gunpowder for the Confederacy.* The execution is thought to have taken place at the cave and was accomplished by hanging.

Several versions of the Sullivan story exist. Whether the victim of the execution was Stephen H. Sullivan Sr. or Stephen Sullivan Jr. is unclear. It may also be that the Stephen Sullivan who was hanged, survived the ordeal by some strange quirk of fate. One version of the tale related in 1954 by a great great grandson of Stephen Sullivan, states that Sullivan survived for a time because a slave quickly cut him down. Sullivan never fully recovered and died about three months later.**

A monument to Stephen and Dorcas Sullivan was erected shortly after the turn of the century by family descendents. Their burial site was once a quiet spot beyond the city limits of Sullivan but has since been swallowed up in modern residential growth. The monument, however, still stands.

Stephen Sullivan may have also contributed to his execution by virtue of his outspoken nature. He was a strong advo-

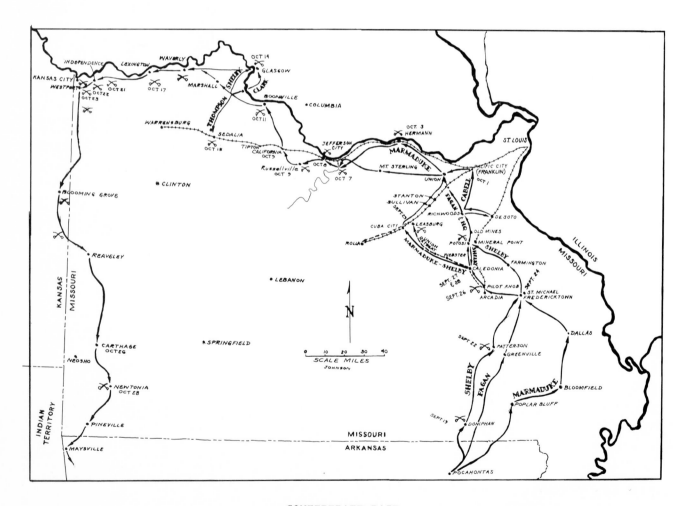

CONFEDERATE RAID
Map showing the path of General Sterling Price's Raid
through Missouri. September-October-November, 1864.

cate of the southern cause and like the south, lost all. The war took his sons, his negroes, his live stock, the merchandise from his general store, his wagons, teams, provisions and money. Sullivan had become a broken man. In the end, the war took his spirit as well as his life.+

In 1864 General Sterling Price staged a raid through Franklin County. Sterling Price, Governor of Missouri from 1853 to 1857, was an active political figure in the state before the war. The approach of the war changed Price from a moderate compromiser into a militant pro-southerner. By March of 1862 Price had left the state to fight for the Confederacy. Although he won no accolades from the West Pointers in the Confederate Army, he was a hero to the guerrillas and southern sympathizers who usually peopled his command.

By 1863 and early 1864 when the Missouri Militia had driven most of the Confederates from the state, the number of Federal troops was considerably reduced. It was at this time that Sterling Price staged a raid through Missouri, his second and most notorious attack. He came into Missouri from Arkansas through the southeast part of the state, defeated Federal troops at Pilot Knob, and moved into Franklin County where he stayed for four days while preparing to move on west in an effort to capture Jefferson City, a task he later did not seriously attempt.

Sullivan was the rendezvous of the 63rd Enrolled Missouri Militia and other military organizations in 1864. It was for this reason that Sterling Price spent considerable time in the area. During his four day stay some 60 local men were killed by his troops and nearly $500,000 in personal property was destroyed.‡

Surviving fragments of stories related to this period of history provide a good basis for speculation regarding the chain of events centered upon the cave's munitions plant.

It was established by Peter Stanton in the 1850's. The Sullivans joined the operation at the outset of the Civil War but the declining influence of the southern sympathizers of the area brought Federal troops down upon the gunpowder operation and Stephen Sullivan may have been executed during this raid.

Slaves quartered at the cave suddenly found themselves free of overseers and in confusion. A portion of the volatile munitions plant blew up. The Federals began patrolling the Freemont Trail and the surviving Confederate sympathizers avoided the cave, refusing to acknowledge or lay claim to their property there, the blacks included.

FOUNDERS GRAVESTONE
The gravestone of Stephen and Dorcas Sullivan. The reverse side states, "Founders of Sullivan, Mo. 1858. It is located in southeast Sullivan, along a residential street.

One source says that "The Union Army utilized the caverns as a gunpowder mill" during the interim period of 1862 and 1864;* however, a prominent authority on saltpetre mining during the Civil War states that the north, having no need for the crude gunpowder produced by these backwoods operations, initiated "destructive action toward such installations rather than recognition and utilization of a valuable source of raw material."‡‡ The presence of Federal patrols along the Freemont Trail near the cave probably gave rise to the rumors that they were making use of the munitions plant themselves.

Sterling Price marched into Franklin County on September 30, 1864 and engaged Federal troops. The Union men taking temporary refuge near Saltpeter Cave were shot or captured and a company of Price's men, participating in their general "pillage, plunder and burn" policy, wrecked havoc at the cave. Their destructiveness was so complete, the gunpowder plant was leveled. With this action the 144-year history of saltpetre mining at Saltpeter Cave came to a close. And it was also this action, say persistent legends, that introduced Jesse James to Saltpeter Cave. On that eventful occasion he is said to have been riding with Quantrill's Irregulars and that on that date, Quantrill was with General Sterling Price.

31

PROCLAMATION
OF THE
GOVERNOR OF MISSOURI!

REWARDS
FOR THE ARREST OF
Express and Train Robbers.

STATE OF MISSOURI,}
EXECUTIVE DEPARTMENT.

WHEREAS, It has been made known to me, as the Governor of the State of Missouri, that certain parties, whose names are to me unknown, have confederated and banded themselves together for the purpose of committing robberies and other depredations within this State, and

WHEREAS, Said parties did, on or about the Eighth day of October, 1879, stop a train near Glendale, in the county of Jackson, in said State, and, with force and violence, take, steal and carry away the money and other express matter being carried thereon; and

WHEREAS, On the fifteenth day of July, 1881, said parties and their confederates did stop a train upon the line of the Chicago, Rock Island and Pacific Railroad, near Winston, in the County of Daviess, in said State, and, with force and violence, take, steal, and carry away the money and other express matter being carried therein; and, in perpetration of the robbery last aforesaid, the parties engaged therein did kill and murder one WILLIAM WESTFALL, the conductor of the train, together with one JOHN McCULLOCH, who was at the time in the employ of said company, then on said train; and

WHEREAS, FRANK JAMES and JESSE W. JAMES stand indicted in the Circuit Court of said Daviess County, for the murder of JOHN W. SHEETS, and the parties engaged in the robberies and murders aforesaid have fled from justice and have absconded and secreted themselves;

NOW, THEREFORE, in consideration of the premises, and in lieu of all other rewards heretofore offered for the arrest or conviction of the parties aforesaid, or either of them, by any person or corporation, I, THOMAS T. CRITTENDEN, Governor of the State of Missouri, do hereby offer a reward of five thousand dollars, ($5,000.00) for the arrest and conviction of each person participating in either of the robberies or murders aforesaid, excepting the said FRANK JAMES and JESSE W. JAMES; and for the arrest and delivery of said

FRANK JAMES and JESSE W. JAMES,

and each or either of them, to the sheriff of said Daviess County, I hereby offer a reward of five thousand dollars, ($5,000.00,) and for the conviction of either at the parties last aforesaid of participation in either of the murders or robberies above mentioned, I hereby offer a further reward of five thousand dollars, ($5,000.00.)

IN TESTIMONY WHEREOF, I have hereunto set my hand and caused to be affixed the great Seal of the State of Missouri. Done

[SEAL.] at the City of Jefferson on this 28th day of July, A. D. 1881.

THOS. T. CRITTENDEN.

By the Governor:
MICH'L K. McGRATH, Sec'y of State.

PROCLAMATION OF THOMAS T. CRITTENDEN.
GOVERNOR OF MISSOURI.

THE LEGENDARY JESSE JAMES

The James Home as it appeared in 1934.

(Courtesy-State Historical Society of Missouri)

Legends provide much of the romance of history and there are few more colorful, daring and adventuresome than those about Jesse James, the "Robin Hood of Americana."

Many Ozark caves are reputed to have once been a Jesse James hideout. Only a few caves were probably authentic links in the escape routes utilized by the James-Younger Gang when fleeing authorities of law and order. Less than half a dozen of these cave hideout legends are probably true oral traditions dating to the 1870's.

Only one Missouri cave, Meramec Caverns (Saltpeter Cave), has achieved international fame as a legendary hideout of Jesse James. This has largely accrued in modern times because of the cave's popularity as a tourist attraction.

The sources of this legend are vague. References to it predating the 1940's have not been located by this writer. One agent appears to have been Jack Berlin of Indiana. Better known as "Ozark Jack" and reputed to have once been an Indian Scout, Berlin made claims in the 1950's to having been one of Jesse Jame's playmates as a child. In 1950 "Ozark Jack" was an old man gifted at telling tales about his youthful days in the late 1800's. Author Henry J. Walker (1961) recounts a version of the "Ozark Jack" story wherein Jack and two friends happened upon the James Gang at Saltpeter Cave in the fall of 1881. Walker, however, relegates this particular narrative to a chapter titled "Legends and Stories" in his book *Jesse James The Outlaw.* *

For the particulars of the Meramec Caverns legend about Jesse James we must turn to Lester B. Dill, the owner and operator of the cave since 1933.

According to Mr. Dill, the James Brothers became familiar with the cave while riding with Quantrill's Irregulars during the Civil War. The introduction came during the Franklin County raid in 1864 by General Sterling Price. Quantrill, legend purports, was riding with General Price at the time. "Jesse and his brother Frank were both members of the Quantrill Irregulars" Dill says, "and as such took part in the demolition of the...Powder Mill. This enabled Jesse to study and remember the...passageways to the caverns, a knowledge he was to use later, to good advantage, during his career as a bank and train robber.

"This began during the 1870's when Jesse James and his notorious gang of outlaws frequently used Meramec Caverns as a hideout. The cave was particularly adapted to his purpose because his entire band could gallop at full speed right into its depths, thus affording a baffling shield from troublesome posses and government pursuers. It was in Meramec Caverns that Jesse is said to have frequently divided the loot obtained from his numerous excursions into outlawry." **

33

Jesse Woodson James was born September 5, 1847 in Clay County, Missouri to Rev. Robert and Zerelda Cole James. Destined to achieve infamy even before he reached adulthood, Jesse James became a legend in his own time.

When Civil War came to Missouri in 1862 Jesse was too young for enlistment but his older brother Frank was 19 and immediately rode off to join the guerrilla band led by William Clark Quantrill. Riding with Frank was Cole Younger, a cousin.

By 1864 Jesse had turned 17 years of age. He promptly followed in his brothers footsteps and enlisted with Quantrill. He joined in time to participate in Quantrill's bloody raid on Lawrence, Kansas. During the assult many unarmed persons were massacred. Jesse had his first taste at spilling human blood.

The war, as fought along the Missouri-Kansas border, was bloody. It was also bitter. Frank, Jesse and Cole, riding under the leadership of Quantrill and "Bloody" Bill Anderson, acquired such an unsavory reputation, Jesse's parents were banished from the state by Union soldiers.

For a brief period immediately following the end of the war, Union soldiers hunted Quantrill's guerrillas with vengence. Regular southern soldiers had been

pardoned. The guerrillas were considered outlaws.

The vendetta was short lived. A general amnesty for guerrillas was soon issued. Military and political leaders hoped that amnesty would end all hostilities. But fate decreed otherwise.

Jesse, Frank and Cole Younger, hearing of the amnesty, came out of hiding and rode toward Lexington, Missouri, but were intercepted by a company of Union soldiers who disregarded the white flag of truce Jesse James carried and attacked. The trio escaped but in the hail of gunfire Jesse received a serious chest wound.

Jesse survived his painful injury but spent two years agonizing his way back to health. During this time his name faded from the lips of most people, even his enemies. That respite ended on February 13, 1866 when the Clay County Savings Bank at Liberty, Missouri, was robbed of $60,000. Participants included Frank James and Cole Younger. The James-Younger Gang had been born.

In October of 1866 the Lexington, Missouri bank was robbed by the same gang. Riding beside Frank and Cole was Jesse.

Men who rode on into Missouri's early outlaw history at the side of Frank and

JESSE WOODSON JAMES
Last picture taken before his death.
(Courtesy-State Historical Society
of Missouri)

FRANK JAMES AT 55
(Courtesy-State Historical Society
of Missouri)

Jesse James were former associates during the war. They include, among others, Jim Younger, Thomas Little, Payton Jones, Ed and Clell Miller, Charlie Pitts, George and Oliver Shepherd, Dick Burns, Andy McGuire and Arch Clements.

Robberies committed by the James-Younger Gang were staged in Kentucky, Iowa, Arkansas, and Minnesota as well as Missouri. Their unhealthy influence spread, eventually breeding other malevolent gangs led by such outlaws as Belle and Henry Starr, Grat and Emmett Dalton, Al and Frank Jennings, Bill Cook and Ben Howell.

In January of 1874 the James-Younger Gang staged a train robbery at Gads Hill, Missouri. The outlaws captured a small whistlestop of a town and robbed the incoming Iron Mountain Express, netting $2,000.

Gads Hill is located approximately seventy-five miles south and east of Meramec Caverns. It was this robbery which Lester B. Dill says brought the James-Younger Gang back to their old Civil War haunt--Saltpeter Cave.

After the train robbery, Dill says "the gang was tracked to the caverns by a posse; and after a seige of three days, they escaped by an unknown route..."*

Dill maintains that the secret exit was made by following the course of the cave's underground stream to its resurgence just north of the cave's large entrance. Guides, explaining this sequence of events to modern day visitors, relate that the posse, upon entering the cave, were puzzled to find the outlaws' horses milling about in the dark of the cave near a pool of water. This "pool" was in reality a "low dip" in the cave passage where water collected, creating an inverted siphon. It cleverly concealed a continuation of the cave. Apparently the gang knew that more passageway existed beyond the siphon and some observers believe that during the Civil War period when the munitions plant at the cave was making generous use of the cave's water supply, the water level in the pool was lower, thereby making the cave's more remote portions common knowledge to those who entered it.**

Jesse James's outlaw career ended on the morning of April 3, 1882 at St. Joseph, Missouri--shot in the head by Robert Ford. In a moment of carelessness, and in the presence of a traitorous gang member, Jesse had laid his guns aside.

The manner of Jesse's death through a cowards treachery, strengthened the Jesse James legend. In the decades that followed, his legend grew even greater. That

BLOODY BILL ANDERSON
Outlaw Leader

(Courtesy- State
Historical Society
of Missouri)

BLOODY BILL ANDERSON
After death

legend is still alive and championed as strongly today as ever. Even his death has come to be questioned. Some firmly believe that he was not killed on that fateful day in April of 1882, and that an imposter was lowered into the grave, and, that Jesse survived to a ripe old age under an assumed name.

    Perhaps.

We will study the Jesse James legend again in this review of the history of Meramec Caverns for in 1949 Jesse and all the romance of his legend was reborn at Meramec Caverns. It was a unique event in the annuals of American cave history.

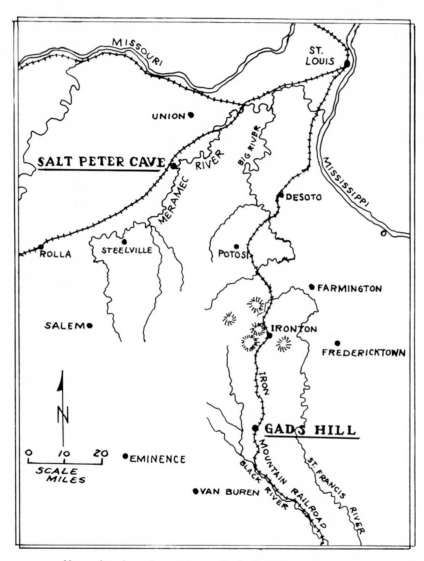

Map showing location of Gads Hill, Missouri and its relationship to Meramec Caverns.

THE RAILROAD AND RICHES

The settlement of Franklin County and the region along the spring-fed Meramec River near Saltpeter Cave began even before the Louisiana Purchase in 1802. The county was officially organized in December of 1818. Its growth was piecemeal until the coming of the railroad in the 1850's, whereupon, the county's economic growth developed in leaps and bounds. For the first time the county's agricultural and mineral wealth could be shipped to market easily and economically.

Missouri's first railroad, the Missouri Pacific, moved westward from St. Louis to St. Joseph in 1851. West of Franklin County the Iron Mountain Express began to operate. And in 1858-1859, the San Francisco Railroad tracked its way into Franklin County, going through Stanton and coming within one and a half miles of Saltpeter Cave.

Stanton was a new, lively community, and headquarters of the Stanton Copper Mines.

Common business and political interests created a bond of partnership between the Stanton and Sullivan families. Already John and Peter Stanton, and Stephen Sullivan had investigated the possibilities for reactivating the munitions plant at Saltpeter Cave.

The cave's rightful owner was Charles J. Carpenter of St. Louis. He had acquired the 48.29 acres of land upon which the cave lay as a government land grant in November of 1850.* His acquisition may have been for purposes of mineral specu-

lation as the land was not suitable for cultivation. Its only visible assets other than its mineral potential was timber. If the Stantons and Sullivans negotiated a legal agreement with Carpenter for rights to the cave's saltpeter reserves, there is no visible record. Carpenter's relationship to the saltpeter enterprise is presently unknown.

Until word came that a railroad was to be routed through Franklin County, Stephen and Dorcas Sullivan had lived along the banks of the Meramec River downstream from Saltpeter Cave at Hamilton Ford. Mr. Sullivan saw opportunity in railroad construction. He "took his force of negroes and white men...and went to St. Louis, camped at Chouteau Pond, cut the right of way, made ties for the Pacific Railroad to Franklin, now called Pacific, which was the end of the road for several years.

"They then surveyed and built the South West Branch, now the Frisco, to Rolla. When they began to build from Franklin, Mr. Sullivan again took his force of hands, cut the right of way and made ties for the railroad, to this point, taking the profit of his contract in stock in the railroad, which amounted to several thousand dollars, and a pass for himself and family for life... On arriving at this point (site of

C. A. RUEPPELE at age 32
(Courtesy- Washington, Mo. Public Library)

replaced by the appearance of the Schmukes and Rueppeles.

According to Ida Schmuke of Stanton "the Rueppele family came to St. Louis with the Busche family with whom Charles Rueppele was close. They encouraged his interests around Stanton. He struck it good in iron and sulphur mining."◊

Originally of Norweign stock, most of the Rueppele family lived in Germany.◊◊

In his 40's upon arrival in the New World, Charles Rueppele, backed by his St. Louis friends, did well from the beginning. He began dealing in real estate, buying Atlantic and Pacific Railroad property for 50¢ to $1.00 per acre.‡ His land transactions between 1872 and 1895 were volumnous and profitable.‡‡ Between 1878 and 1895, the year of his death, his land holdings were valued at $25,000.‡

PLAT OF STANTON, MISSOURI
Circa 1900

modern day Sullivan),the surveyors informed Mr. Sullivan that this point...was so geographically situated that it was destined to make a commercial city, and that it was the first chance for a city of any consequence this side of St. Louis. Mr. Sullivan immediately bought the land, surveyed it, laid out and founded the town...and moved here from the Meramec... in 1858."+

The mining of lead, iron, zinc and copper continued after the Civil War, as a strong economic base for the Sullivan-Stanton communities. Numerous blast furnaces were put into operation. Until the general panic of 1877-1878, large quantities of lead was mined and pig iron manufactured.

Not until the 1880's did the town of Sullivan truly begin to prosper. The community of Stanton, however, started to decline as a center of commerce. *Campbell's Gazateer of Missouri* for 1874 lists Stanton as having three stores in addition to a Post Office. Sullivan, in the same directory, was given only two stores.++

The influence of the Stanton family also declined in the 1870's and 1880's,

Charles (C.A.) Rueppele (Jr.) was born in 1866 and inherited his father's holdings in 1895.‡‡His interests in mining were greater than his father's and C.A. prospered in earnest. His land holdings in and about Stanton were extensive and he eventually acquired the property beneath which lay Saltpeter Cave. This occurred before 1898. To the day of his death in 1934 he was convinced that valuable mineral deposits existed on the cave property.

The 1898 Plat of the Town of Stanton shows the extent of the Rueppele real estate. Other residents who owned considerable plots of land on both sides of the St. Louis and San Francisco railroad tracks that bisected the town north to south, were the Gideons and Schmukes. All three families (Rueppeles, Gideons and Schmukes) were destined to become a part of the history of Saltpeter Cave as the 19th Century faded into the 20th.

D. N. Gideon General Merchandise Store, Stanton, Mo. (Courtesy- Elmer Gowan)

THE OLD HAMMER STORE, STANTON, MO.
A prominent early day landmark.
(Courtesy- Ida Schmuke)

DANCES AND DISCOVERY

Group gathering for party at Salt Peter Cave.
Circa. 1910   (Courtesy - Ida Schmuke)

Great advances took place in education and in the arts in the decade after the Civil War. Missouri, like the rest of the nation, experienced tremendous cultural growth. People looked forward to the turn of the century with enthusiasm and optimism. It was one of the happiest periods in American history and none of those years were more frivolous than the "Gay 90's." For the people of the Stanton and Sullivan communities it was the age of lavish "cave parties" of the like not seen elsewhere in rural Missouri. And Saltpeter Cave was, once again, a hub of community action.

The town of Stanton had two general stores, one fronting Elliot Street on the west side of the tracks, and the second fronting Springfield Avenue on the east side of the tracks.* One of these was operated by D. N. Gideon who listed his occupation as grocer.**

Visitors arriving by train found three buildings facing the Train Depot to the west. One was a hotel, the second a saloon, and the third was a dance hall. All three buildings were on Wurzburger land but the hotel and saloon were operated by Joseph Schmuke who preferred to be known as a hotel man.+ Much of the time, the saloon was tended by John Door whose home was on the east side of the tracks about one and a half blocks away.++

On Friday and Saturday nights Stanton was a lively place. The proximity of the Dance Hall to the saloon was ideal. It led to noisy frivolity and even drunken brawls. Troublesome fights might wreck the saloon or boil over into the dusty street next to the Train Depot.◊

Typical of many small villages in those days, the saloon keeper was often the town Marshall. John Door served in this capacity and on one occasion, broke up a fight at the expense of having to have his own stomach stitched back together.◊◊

Summer nights were often hot. The Missouri humidity did not add to comfort. It was under these circumstances one sweaty night that someone suggested they all go down to Saltpeter Cave to cool off. A brawling, excited group of revelers descended upon the quiet old cave, bearing torches, lanterns and candles.

Three-hundred feet inside the cave's spacious entrance passage, the underground corridor opens into a huge chamber large enough to accommodate hundreds of people. Here, the group found the comfort they sought. The cave's limestone walls absorbed their shouts and laughter, and the dirt floor was pounded into a hard-packed surface by many dancing feet. A new tradition had been initiated. Never again would this accommodating natural ballroom be overlooked or neglected. The dance hall in town lost its charm. A new love affair had begun.

Joseph Schmuke and D. N.

41

JOSEPH SCHMUKE
(Courtesy- Ida Schmuke)

D. N. GIDEON
(Courtesy- Washington, Mo. Public Library)

Gideon were quick to take notice of the natural qualities offered by the cave. With the permission of Charles Rueppele, they teamed up to form a dance committee and set about to exploit this newly discovered resource. The Gay 90's were just getting underway and they meant to be in on the ground floor, even if it was underground.

A first order of business was to construct a wooden dance floor within the cave, position lanterns about the chamber for illumination, set candles and lanterns along the entrance corridor to provide light to the inner chamber, clear brush at the cave entrance, dress up the river front before the cave opening, and put the old wagon road going down to the cave in passable shape.

With all of this accomplished, dates were selected for parties, a band of local musicians featuring good fiddlers was retained, and handbills were printed and distributed throughout the area.*

It didn't take long for the news to spread. The Public Relations Department of the Frisco Railroad soon caught wind of the new attraction, presumably through the station master at Stanton, and spread word of the event up and down the tracks from St. Louis to Springfield.

The parties were a grand success from the beginning and hardly a summer weekend went by without some type of sponsored activity at the cave.

When winter rolled around the thought occurred to Schmuke that it might be possible to cut ice on the river during the cold months, store the ice inside the cave, and have it for the following spring and summer to cool drinks at the dances. A large quantity of ice was cut from the Meramec River that winter and stored back within the cave. But as luck would have it, Schmuke did not insulate the ice well enough and by spring all of it had melted. Disappointed and not wishing to go to the trouble and expense of collecting ice again, he forewent this bold scheme. But the dances continued.

D. N. Gideon and Joseph Schmuke sponsored many summer dances and picnics at the cave between 1895 and 1910. They even saw to the construction of a second dance floor at the cave, this one near the spring along the bluff just downstream from the cave entrance.**

Traffic from St. Louis was often substantial. Ida Schmuke, still residing at Stanton, and a daughter-in-law of Joseph Schmuke, says "In 1900 people came out from St. Louis by train and then were taken down to the river and cave in a wagon with seats. The cave parties were well attended."+

Eddie Door of Virden, Illinois, a son of John Door, says "My Dad got involved with the dances because he worked for Mr. Schmuke. You could drive a team and wagon into the cave in those days and Dad often took people from Stanton down to the cave. Sometimes he'd take them clear back inside to where the dance floor was. If it was a hot night, he'd leave the team near the cave entrance where it was cool and there was a spring they could drink from."++

In the summer of 1904 a stranger came to town. On board the train he had heard about the cave and the big parties held there. At Schmuke's Saloon he learned considerably more.

No one knew the gentleman but he seemed to be a very friendly, open, likable chap. He had wealthy business partners in St. Louis, so everyone seemed to think. His dashing appearance, expensive clothing, impecable manners and gifted way of speaking impressed all who met him.

The stranger made a trip to the cave to inspect its facilities. Later he let it be known that he was looking for just such a place to develop into a resort. Saltpeter Cave, he claimed, was that for which he was looking. And he also let it

be known that although most of the stock for the new development was owned by his business partners, there was still some left for those who might wish to invest.

It did not take a degree in math to fathom the economics of this opportunity. Anyone who had ever attended one of the Saturday night dances could see how popular the cave site was.

To "salt his mine" so to speak, the stranger announced grandiose plans for the cave and river front. The company was also going to develop a rail line from Stanton to the cave so that visitors could ride the three miles in comfort. To make it look good he had a train car load of rails and ties shipped to Stanton and parked on a track siding.

A "tie laying" ceremony to inaugurate the development was planned for July 4th. Where the tracks were to begin, an archway decorated with colorful wrappings was erected.

Scores of people invested in the new enterprise. The amount of money collected by the stranger for his "bogus" stock is reported to have been several thousand dollars. Charles Rueppele is said to have been one of the few individuals that did not actually invest hard cash. He owned the cave property and stood to harvest a

Tie Laying Ceremony, Stanton, Mo., July 4, 1904
(Courtesy- Ida Schmuke)

Tie Laying Ceremony, Stanton, Mo., July 4, 1904
(Courtesy- Ida Schmuke)

sizable sum of money on a lease arrangement for the cave.

On the appointed day, a lively crowd gathered at the "tie laying" site. A photographer was also on hand. But the stranger was not. To their dismay, the investors soon learned that the stranger had absconded with their money, having fled south via the same rails that brought him. He was never seen again.*

Saltpeter Cave was not, of course, the only cave at which "cave parties" were conducted. Green's Cave and Fisher's Cave, both upstream from Saltpeter Cave, were party sites. While the Gideons and Schmukes sponsored gala events at Saltpeter, the Sullivan family of Sullivan, and the Schwarzers and Bienkes of Washington, Missouri, encouraged activities at Fisher's Cave.

"Cave parties are numerous these days," said the *Sullivan Sentinel* in July of 1901. "The Hinchcliff crowd to the number of 21 went in two wagons to Fisher's Cave last Saturday and made a deal of racket, especially as they came through town on the return trip." ¢

Even the St. Louis visitors took in Fisher's Cave. "S. H. Sullivan, Jr. and his sister Neda, were hosts to a party of young people last Saturday who came out from St. Louis on the excursion to Fisher's Cave. They explored the cave thoroughly and took several flashlight pictures..." so reported the local paper in May of 1902.¢¢

Occasionally the crowds were so large special arrangements were necessary. An event at Green's Cave in July of 1903 was typical. Sixty St. Louisians were involved and "had a car (railroad) chartered for their special and exclusive use... S. H. Sullivan, Jr. had the party."‡

In October of 1905 an even larger event was staged at Fisher's Cave and entertained so many people the local paper declined to list them all by name but reported that at the height of the party "people attending came from Gray Summit, St. Louis, Kansas City (and) Pacific..." The "party lasted for three or four days" and employed "three colored cooks."‡‡

The Franz Schwarzers family of Washington, organized a "cave explorers club" to engage in spelunking and partying at Fisher's Cave and other caves along the Meramec River. It was the first organized cave club in Missouri.‡

Not to be outdone, S. H. Sullivan, Jr. organized a cave club of his own in 1902 at Sullivan. The *Sullivan Sentinel* in June of 1906 reported that "The explorers club, consisting of a jolly lot of young folks of St. Louis, made their 4th Annual trip to Sullivan last Sunday in a special car which was set out for them here. About 40 were in the party this trip and they went out to Marquis Cave on Hamilton Branch for the day. S. H. Sullivan, Jr., the real organizer of the club, had general charge of the party after they arrived in Sullivan and with his sister Neda, Sullivan made the trip a most enjoyable one for the party. They made the trip out to the cave on two hay frames with a two-horse wagon to carry provisions... They expect to explore the Saltpeter Cave on their next trip... They all wore badges with the wording EXPLORERS CLUB, SULLIVAN, MISSOURI, JUNE 3, 1906."*

John Sullivan, a descendent of S. H. Sullivan, Jr., and still a resident of Sullivan, has among his many momentos of the past, one of these treasured badges worn by S. H. Sullivan, Jr.**

It was inevitable that this emphasis upon cave exploration would result in new discoveries. A major find was made at Saltpeter Cave in the summer of 1901.

"The party which went to Saltpeter Cave last week found a new cave, or rather an extension of the Saltpeter Cave." reported the local paper. "This cave has always been considered a short one, but the boys took an old ax and chopped out a small hole at the end of the left hand prong and it opened into a large chamber. This extended with much winding and uneveness for a long distance, some of the party said a mile and a half. The scenery is very rugged and exceedingly beautiful, never having been molested by destructive curiousity seekers, as all the previously known caves in the region have been."+

Saltpeter Cave opens to the east, its entrance an imposing arched opening 50 feet wide and 20 feet high. Its entrance corridor penetrates the hill for some 300 feet in a westerly direction, then curves left to become a large chamber known as "The Ballroom." This spacious underground void is circular in shape, even-floored, more than 100 feet across and 40 feet high at the center.

From "The Ballroom," the cave continues as a series of three more chambers of diminishing size. At this point the cave passage had all the appearance of a "fork" in the early days, the division created by boulders of stone, large and complex "spongework" cavities in the limestone, and the configuration of the passage cross section.

To the left, the passage appeared to dead end in spongework tubes. To the right the ceiling descended rapidly and

THE BALLROOM
Early photograph of "The Ballroom" showing the fenced in dance floor.
(Courtesy-Meramec Caverns)

45

THE WINE TABLE
Early view of the "Wine Table" room. Note stalagmites
on the floor of the chamber and on top of the "table".
(Courtesy- Ida Schmuke)

seemed to literally disappear into a pool of standing water. Here, for all practical purposes, the big cave was thought to end.

A secret guarded by the cave since the pre-Civil War days when a munitions plant functioned within the cavern was, that beyond the quiet, spring-fed pool, a large and colorful portion of the cave stretched for several miles along an underground river--the source of the spring which emerged near the cave's entrance. Only Jesse James knew the secret of the pool and he had imparted this knowledge to no one.outside the members of his gang.

During the era of the gala cave parties no one probed this cold, mysterious pool of water referred to as "the pond." But energetic members of the S. H. Sullivan, Jr.'s cave exploring club did poke about in the cavities along the walls of the left fork. While thus engaged, a small hole was found which opened to blackness beyond. A strong current of air also poured through the gap and this raised suspicions of more cave beyond. The old ax was brought forward and a new discovery made.

The wonders they beheld were breath-taking. For the first time human eyes swept up and over the massive bulk of "Onyx Mountain," one of America's largest stalagmite structures. And behind it lay an alcove where onyx flowstone glittered with a jewel-like, pure white surface. A spring, cascading down over the rimstone terraces ended in a reflective pool studded with onyx columns, stalactites and stalagmites.

Leaving this area the explorers followed a narrow, winding, barren passage that would come to be known as "Depression Alley," and found their way onward and upward into even higher levels beneath the earth. Magnificent complexes of cave formations greeted their curious eyes at almost every turn.

Finally, reaching what is today called the "Fourth Level," the happy explorers entered a large chamber to discover the "Stage Curtains." They had indeed found America's finest cave scene.

Joseph Schmuke was thrilled with the new discoveries. Another cave party was planned immediately, and the news release that appeared in the local paper following the event, carried a prophetic message.

46

"A picnic was given at Saltpeter Cave last Sunday, Joseph Schmuke and John Door committee on arrangements. Considerable money and time were spent in preparing for the picnic and making it possible to explore the new addition to the cave recently discovered. Ladders and bridges were placed wherever necessary, making it possible for women and children to see the magnificent beauty of the place. Too much cannot be said in commendation of the enterprise shown by these men. The place-- the cave, spring, grove and river--is worthy of a wider reputation than it now has..."+

Thirty-two years later Lester B.Dill, a native of the Stanton community, commercialized Saltpeter Cave and called it Meramec Caverns. Dill was destined to fulfill the prophesy of 1901 regarding "a wider reputation" for the grand old cave. By the middle of the 20th century Meramec Caverns would not only be Missouri's most popular cave attraction, but one of the world's most famous underground wonders. Young and old throughout the world would come to recognize Meramec Caverns not only for its beauty, but its history as the legendary hideout of Jesse James, the "Robinhood of Americana."

PICNIC POSTER
An original poster for a cave picnic,
May 18,1895. (Photo by Weaver)

PART II
A MAN NAMED BILL

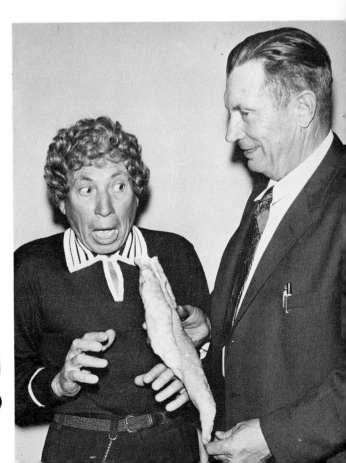

49

SAVED BY SMOKE

The boys were lost in Onyx Cave and they were getting the shakes. It had not been their idea in the first place but rather the urging of the youngest member of the group, Lester B. Dill.

The year was 1909. Les was eleven years old. Already he was gifted with a persuasive tongue which most of his playmates admired but his mother disdained. Les, like Tom Sawyer, was a boy with "adventuresome, troublesome ways." One fact was plain and simple. He liked caves.

Other boys gravitated to Les as if a powerful magnet was hidden on his person. It was a frequent vexation to the mothers of his friends because they knew, as did their youngsters, that wherever Les Dill was, excitement and adventure was just around some corner.

If this worried the adults, it certainly did not worry the young boys that lived on the farms in the Valley of the Meramec. If Les Dill thought something was worth doing, the other youngsters usually agreed. But even getting lost in Onyx Cave didn't destroy their faith in him. It was a scary thing, but Les would find a way out.

The group of youngsters had ventured into the cave armed with a kerosene lamp and some candles they had filched from the picnic site along the river. Earlier in the day they had all been in attendance at a big Sunday picnic sponsored by the church to which their folks belonged. The boys seldom laid claim to being church members, leastwise not to each other. They considered themselves victims of circumstances.

Everything had gone along fine until the lantern had run out of fuel at a place where the cave was becoming complex enough to confuse their sense of direction. It was apparent they were going in circles. So the boys, worried and tired, sat down on the chilly, wet, limestone boulders that littered the floor. The mud was of no consequence as they were already smeared with that from head to toe.

"What do we do now?" one boy asked.

"Maybe we ought to find the cave stream" another suggested.

A third boy, less self confident and more fragile in stature, began to whimper. Earlier he had stumbled and fallen. Fatigue and fright distorted his imagination. He viewed the whole ordeal fatalistically.

To bolster their self confidence several older boys produced some tobacco and cigarette papers. One could always think better over a smoke, or so it seemed. They rolled cigarettes and offered their companions an opportunity to partake of this forbidden pleasure.

Les Dill, concealing the fact that this was one wickedness in which he had not

LESTER B. DILL
A legend in his own time.

had a chance to indulge, took the prof-fered tobacco and rolled himself a crude cigarette. Nursing the smoke, as he had seen adults do, he puffed away while pond-ering their plight. It occurred to him that his mother might tan his hide if she smelled tobacco smoke on his breath, but, if they got out of the cave alive, she'd probably be so thankful she'd over-look this one moment of weakness.

Eleven years old, smoking for the first time, and fascinated by the morbid nature of their circumstances, Les Dill sat in the spooky, dim light of a candle and "watched the smoke drifting away through chilly tunnels. He exhaled again, watched as that puff too danced away on the draft--and thought of the hillside air currents that had attracted his chums to the secret cave entrance.

"Lester Dill then made his first gen-eral announcement to any party of spelunk-ers: "Boys, I've got it!"

"At that moment..., Dill did have it--a saving touch of mastery and luck...* He noticed that the smoke was being blown in a certain direction, obviously by an air current, and the air could only come from the outside.

He told his companions that if they followed the air currents, they would find the exit. With what they considered wicked delight, the boys quite literally smoked their way out of the cave!**

   ★   ★   ★

For Lester B. Dill, Onyx Cave was truly the beginning of a life-long adven-ture underground. No other person has pursued caves with as much persistence, dedication and success.

"I have been interested in caves and rocks and nature ever since I can remem-ber," Dill says. "It started when I was six years old and my father took me to Fisher's Cave. A few years later, I per-suaded a group of boys to explore Onyx Cave. They said all right, if I went in first. So I did and that's when we got lost.

"You wouldn't think I would have gone in any more caves, but I did. That ex-perience convinced me you couldn't ever really get lost in a cave. I pestered my teachers and everybody else for more in-formation on caves."+

Persistence paid off. . Mated with Dill's remarkable imagination, gifted a-bilities, promotional genius, and incred-ible luck, he was America's most success-ful commercial caveman by the age of 40. His success is the story of Meramec Caverns in the 20th century.

52

LESTER LEARNS AT FISHERS CAVE

Lester B. Dill was born November 28, 1898 in St. Louis, to Thomas Benton and Daisey (Crockett) Dill. He was the second of nine children, the first, Hugh Dill, having been born in 1897. Later siblings included Daisey, 1901; Leonard, 1904; Raymond, 1907; Orvial, 1910; Virginia, 1914; Ollie, 1917; and Kenneth, 1919.

Thomas Benton, having been born and raised in the Valley of the Meramec, had moved to St. Louis prior to Lester's birth to follow the construction trade; and to make use of his talents as a carpenter. Initially, the opportunities offered by the city seemed promising, but Benton's fortunes were not sustaining. With the birth of his second child, he packed up and returned his family to the soil of his childhood--the rich bottomlands along the Meramec River near where highway 185 now crosses that stream. Eventually, he came to own many acres of good farmland in the valley along the river, a portion of Franklin County now within the boundaries of Meramec State Park.

Among neighbors were the Fishers, Coebrants, Pickles, Daces and Hanbys.

Life on the farm was not easy, but it was healthy and character building. Les Dill, recalling those times says "I worked my head off when I was a boy. When I was a kid I could drive a team of mules all day long and still have energy enough left at the end of the day to go out looking for excitement." And with a grin he will add "those mules would get tired about noon. Good thing to, or else we never would have had a break."*

Dill's first introduction to caves came at the age of six when his father took him to Fisher's Cave across the river from the family farm. Fisher's Cave was then the most popular of the many caves located in the valley.

Plowing in the hot fields had its diversions. "People would come out from St. Louis during the summer months" Les recalls, "to fish and swim or go boating on the river. They heard about Fisher's Cave and they would tie up their boats and walk across the field to talk my Dad into being their guide because they wanted to see Fisher's Cave. I got to be old enough--when I was ten--and Dad would send me with them. The people would usually pay me something.

"Leo Fisher had charge of the cave in those days and he permitted me to use the cave trips to make small change. When my brothers Huge and Leonard helped me, we shared the money.

"I had several lanterns to use for trips into the cave and I kept them near the cave entrance in a box I made about 1911 or 1912.

"Some places in the cave were muddy. The first board walks were laid down in 1865 for a Governor's Inaugural Ball. We had to lay new ones down when I started taking

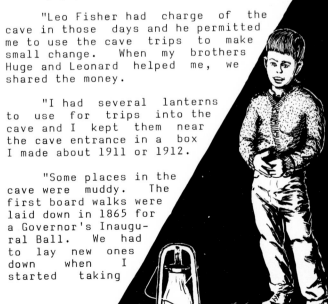

53

FISHERS CAVE
Early scenic view in Fishers Cave 1932
(Courtesy-Halliday, photo by Neville)

In 1888, a description of the cave appeared in a history of Franklin County.◌

Leo and Henry Fisher, commonly referred to as "the Fisher Brothers" were owners of the cave property before the turn of the century;◌◌ however, the Fisher after whom the cave takes its name was an earlier Franklin County settler who owned the cave in 1818.‡ This Fisher, whose first name is said to have been Alexander, was not related to the Fisher Brothers.

In print, the cave is variously referred to as "Fisher", "Fishers", or "Fisher's" cave.

W. D. Sprinkle, a property owner to the south, became an owner of the cave property after the year 1900 and during the early part of the twentieth century, the cave was spoken of as being "on the Sprinkle farm."‡‡

The singular most important ninetieth century event centered about the cave, was a dance held inside the cave in the 1860's

J Harlen Bretz (1956) says "Local historians tell of an Inaugural Ball given by Governor Fletcher in 1865 in the cave's largest room now appropriately called the "Ballroom."‡

people through the cave. The mud would pull ladies' shoes off and I'd then have to put them back on.

"The people I took through actually taught me what to see and talk about on the trips."**

Fisher's Cave, noted earlier as one of the caves from which Renault took saltpetre, has a modest opening no greater in width than 20 feet. Its height is less than 10 feet and the entrance so low in elevation, the cave entrance is impassable when the nearby river is in flood.

The cave has at least 5000 feet of surveyed passage. New discoveries at the cave have been a continuing story since the early 1900's. The most recent outstanding discovery, in 1958, yielded almost 1000 feet of new passage.+ Most early discoveries were made by various members of the Dill family.

First mention of the cave in literature undoubtedly dates to the Civil War for the cave was well known even at that early date. An 1878 reference to the cave noted that the cave "has never been fully explored and though considerably dispoiled by thoughtless adventurers, still contains many beautiful formations and is well worthy of the notice of the curious and the lover of the beautiful."++

GOVERNOR THOMAS C. FLETCHER
(Courtesy- State Historical Society
of Missouri)

54

Thomas C. Fletcher was inaugurated as Governor of Missouri, January 2, 1865, serving until 1869.‡‡ He was the first native born Missourian to hold that office and came from Jefferson County, the county immediately east of Franklin.*

An individual with an obscure past, Fletcher was a member of the Radical Party and very little seems to have been written about him. Why he may have chosen to hold his Inaugural Ball in a cave, if indeed he did, is unknown at this writing.

Oral traditions give two dates for the underground event -- 1865 and 1867. Goodspeed (1888),**a *Centennial History of Sullivan* (1956),+ and a *Historical Review of Franklin County* (1968)++ all mention the event but do not give additional information.

Staging dances at or within caves along the Meramec River is a tradition in the great Valley. It is not unreasonable to believe that a dance was held at Fisher's Cave; however, it seems unlikely that the dance would have been an "Inaugural Ball", particularly when consideration is given to the month in which Fletcher was inaugurated--January--and the remote location of the cave.

Eddie Miller (1974) said "I remember my great grandmother used to talk about seeing people go through Sullivan in buggies on their way to Fisher's Cave to attend Governor Fletcher's Ball."ϕ

According to oral tradition, two large wooden dance-floors and a bandstand were constructed within the cave. The festivities attracted hundreds of people but the ball was short lived. Fumes and smoke from scores of lanterns used for lighting, drove party goers from the cave.‡

Governor Fletcher's Ball is believed to have been the first widely publicized dance ever held in any cave along the Meramec River. Perhaps it was the beginning of the old tradition of underground revelry in the Valley of the Meramec.

FISHERS CAVE
Scenic views in Fishers Cave. (Photos by Weaver)

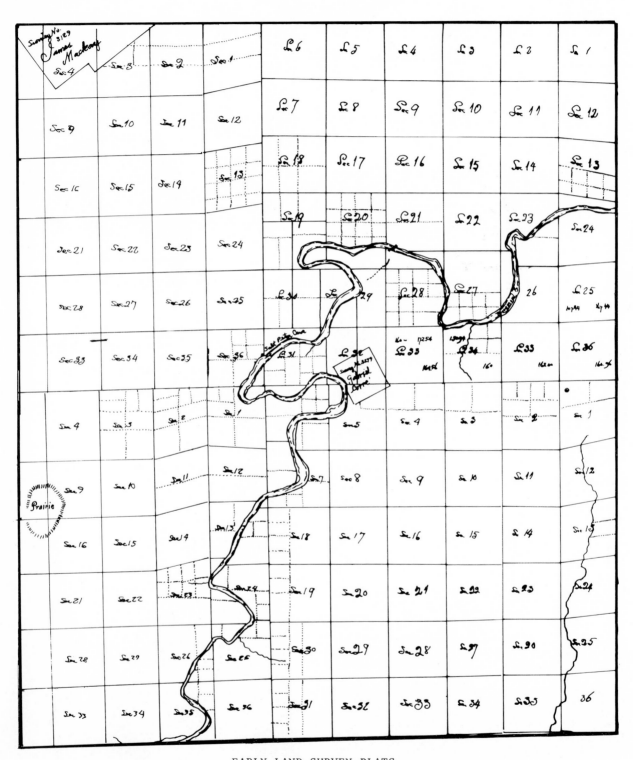

EARLY LAND SURVEY PLATS
This map was drawn from several early land survey plats (1817-1846)
Note Salt Peter Cave notation. (Survey plats from Archives of the
Secretary of State, Jefferson City, Mo.)

DILL PICKLE PARK

Les Dill was preoccupied with caves as a youngster but the idea of showing them to the public as a means of earning money faded with his adolescence. He turned his attentions elsewhere in search of a livelihood following a nine month hitch in the army after graduation from high school.

Les was at home long enough to renew his childhood acquaintance with Mary Hanby, a neighbor girl with whom he had shared his younger years. Both had graduated from the Reedville School. Not only had they played together as children, they had even explored caves together as teenagers.

Changing Mary's last name to Dill, Les took his bride to the oil fields of Oklahoma. He was leaving Fisher's Cave behind but destiny would bring him back. The seeds of his future were already planted there.

"Les followed booms--oil in Oklahoma and Texas, real estate in Florida, rubber in Akron and Dayton, Ohio."*

In the daytime he worked to make a living, and at night he took night school courses to improve his educational background. He studied math and engineering in both Florida and Oklahoma.

After living in Oklahoma for five years and Florida for three, he returned to St. Louis to follow the same trade as his father before him--carpentry.

It was the creation of Meramec State Park near Sullivan that changed every-

thing. It brought germination of the seeds Les had unknowingly planted in the caves of the Meramec Valley.

*   *   *

Legend states that Daniel Boone was first to suggest that the Meramec Valley be preserved.**Most who came after him held similar views. For decades before the creation of Meramec State Park this region was known as "the Playground of St. Louis."

"It was largely through the efforts of Joseph H. Bennett that the area became a state park. It was dedicated on September 8, 1928... Bennett spent many days in Jefferson City in his tireless effort to interest the state in a park in the Meramec Valley."+

Preparations for the park, which was to be the second largest in Missouri, began in 1926.++

The initial tract of land selected comprised 5,778 acres and was consolidated at a cost of $95,220. Acreage was purchased from Leo and Henry Fisher, Mrs. Jane Coebrant, Julian Pickles, W. N.Dace, Mrs. Caledonia and Thomas Benton Dill.

Dill's initial contribution amounted to 290 very choice acres for which he was paid $8,250.¢

The park terrain was described as a "wild, hilly country." At the time of purchase only nine caves were known to exist on the consolidated acreage. It was eventually learned that instead of nine caves, the state owned more than twenty, including the noted Fisher's and Mushroom caves.

There was great public interest in these wild caves. One news reporter wrote "these caves have never been fully explored and their mysteries are yet to be revealed."¢¢

In the year preceding dedication, a name was sought for the new preserve. Missourians were prompted. A flood of proposals came forth. It provided lively newspaper copy through the dull winter months of January, February and March of 1927. Suggested names, among many, included Fisher Cave Park, Martin Park (after pioneer settlers Gus and Frank Martin), Sullivan State Park and Meramec Ozark Park.‡

The Dills have long been noted for their sense of humor. The naming contest was irresistible. In March, readers of the *Sullivan News* were informed that "the *News* has letters from John D. Dill, Maggie L. Dill and Clarence B. Dill...each casting one vote for the "Dill-Pickle State Park" and each giving a good reason for doing so.

THOMAS BENTON DILL
The Yarn-Spinner

"Mr. Dill gave his reason as the natural wish for having something named after an ancestor.

"Mrs. Dill says "My husband John D. Dill was reared on that ground that Thomas Benton Dill sold to the State of Missouri...and played with the little Pickles and the big Pickles when he was a small boy going to school...and none of the names suits any better."

"Clarence B. Dill said "My grandfather Conrad Dill was a pioneer settler in the State of Missouri. My uncle Benton Dill, Conrad Dill's son, sold the land my grandfather settled on."‡‡

The name eventually chosen was Meramec State Park.

Thomas Benton Dill was appointed first Park Superintendent and generally referred to as "Park" or "Refuge Keeper."

Use of the Park began well before roads, camp grounds, river access areas and restroom facilities were complete. This accrued partially from publicity generated by the selection of a name. It seemed as if every visitor wanted at least a brief look at Fisher's Cave also.

Initially, no access road to the cave existed on the west side of the river where the cave opened. Visitors therefore proceeded to the Dill home along the east bank of the river and the Dills had to ferry them across in boats.

"The Park Keeper was kept busy day and night acting as a guide to Fisher Cave and as a bearer of information and as director of camps" reported the local paper for one August weekend during the summer of 1927.≡

Some visitors wanted to see other wild caves of the Park also. Great incentive existed therefore for the Dill family to acquaint themselves with all known caves as well as potential cave areas. In February of 1928 the *Sullivan News* reported:

"Raymond and Hugh Dill (are) going to explore a new cave in the State Park just as soon as weather conditions will permit. At the present time they will have too much water to contend with. Claud Crockett and Raymond Dill made one unfinished trip in this cave which they had to abandon on account of not having sufficient lights. At their destination the cave was 50 feet wide and 16 feet high. It took them five hours to make the round trip. There could be quite a few more caves discovered by opening up the mouths of the numerous springs that are in the park as they all lead to openings in the earth."✱

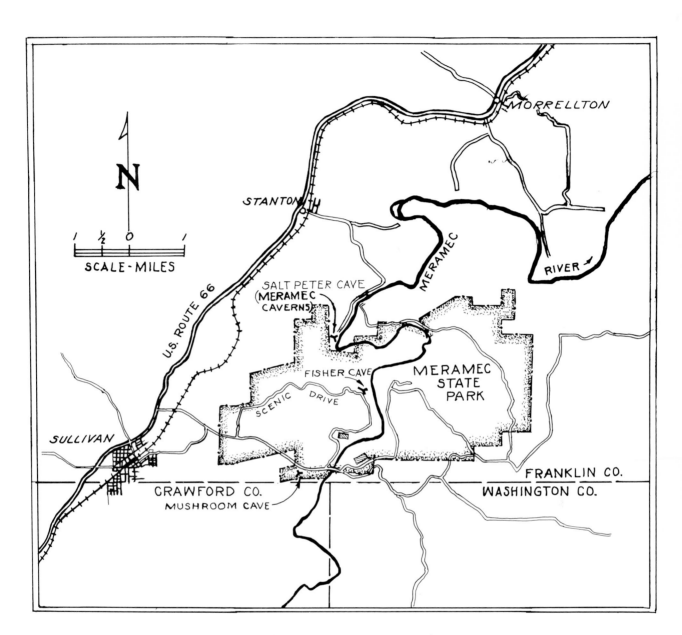

ORIGINAL BOUNDARIES OF MERAMEC STATE PARK

It was this demand for guides that Les answered, assisting his father and brothers in showing Fisher's Cave and other caves in the Park. And so it was that the mysteries of Outlaws' Cave, Bear Cave, Bootleggers' Cave, Shelter Cave, Copper Hollow Cave, Walker Cave, Garrett Cave, Sheep Cave, Wildcat Cave, Fisher's Cave and Mushroom Cave and others were slowly brought to light.

Dedication of the Park came on September 8, 1928. Thousands of people witnessed the ceremony.

"It was fitting," wrote the *St. Louis Globe Democrat* "that the initial words of the dedication should be spoken by Benton Dill, known as philosopher, preacher, musician and Keeper of the Park. He knows almost every foot of its almost 7,000 acres.

"In his dramatic Ozark fashion he urged those that had assembled in the park (that they) should do their share in protecting this gift to the people. "Every acre of this park is sacred to me" Dill said. "These are the scenes of my childhood. I love the wildlife of these hills and valleys, the cool of the springs and caves. God made them for our use and I trust you all will cooperate with me and the other keepers and game wardens so that the beauties of nature may be preserved for you and your children."**

Thomas Benton Dill

MISSOURI MAGAZINE

SQUARE NAILS AND TALL TALES

MUSHROOMS IN MUSHROOM
A. L. Drumeller examining the mushroom beds
in Mushroom Cave, Meramec State Park

Assisting his father on weekends at Fisher's Cave and in Meramec State Park, Les noted that large numbers of people were being attracted to the area. Encouraged by his father, he approached state officials on the possibility of leasing Fisher's and Mushroom caves.

"It took quite a while" Dill says. "We did a lot of dickering but I finally got a signed deal. I promised to pay the state 50 per cent of my net profits. The state, as well as me and my family, were out of luck for almost two years because I didn't have any money to start with."*

Les Dill constructed his own souvenir stands, as well as washrooms, from scrap lumber salvaged from old buildings in the Park.

"It took me more than a year," he says, "to get the caves in good condition and the property improved.

"One big problem was promotion. We weren't allowed to advertise like most tourist attractions because we were located in the State Park. But I knew some newspapermen in St. Louis and they gave me free publicity now and then.

"We charged 50¢ for adults and 25¢ for children. Our soft drinks, food and souvenirs were homemade."**

Les was assisted by several of his brothers, Raymond and Hugh in particular. One or the other usually watched Mushroom Cave while Les operated Fisher's as the principal attraction. Visitors to Fisher's Cave were told about Mushroom Cave while on tour inside Fisher's Cave. Business at Mushroom Cave was largely of a referral nature.

In 1899 H. B. Kerriush of Sullivan raised mushrooms at the cave--hence its unusual name--but ceased his efforts shortly thereafter. He tried his luck again in the period 1922 through 1927 and was more successful, shipping the edible product in 50 pound lots to points as distant as Kansas City and Cincinnati, Ohio.+

Willard "Wes" Hanby of the Sullivan area also tried his hand at mushroom farming at the cave in the early 1900's. Development of the Park brought mushroom farming to an end at Mushroom Cave.++

*   *   *

Fisher's Cave, the most popular of the two caverns, begins as a long, sinuous corridor 600 feet in length. Halfway along this stream-carved course, a broad, low-ceilinged side passage to the left is floored with a "river" of travertine dams. This series of step-like basins of stone, once held water but are dry much of the time today. There are literally hundreds of pockets and rimstone dams, the largest being about four feet in height.

The cave's entrance corridor leads, by way of a ramp and

61

WILLARD WES HANDBY AND HIS WIFE

complex system.

Beyond the "Ballroom", only 700 additional feet was shown commercially in the right hand fork. This portion included the "Grand Canyon", "Ozark Sunset Room", "Devil's Coal Bin", "Old Maid's Room", and "Mohammeds Room". The trail terminated at the "Fountain of Youth".

*   *   *

There were no electric lights in the cave in Dill's day, nor are there now nearly 50 years later. Tours were made using kerosene lanterns which the guides jokingly referred to as "old hay burners". To show total darkness, a traditional part of any cave tour, the lanterns were placed inside a large wooden box which could then be closed for a few minutes.∮

Some of the first money spent by the State of Missouri to promote tourism, it is claimed, was to buy film and take photographs in Fisher's Cave and at Meramec State Park. To accomplish this, pictures were made through time exposure. For lighting, magnesium flares provided the principal illumination and details were "painted in" by lantern light.∮∮

It was at Fisher's Cave that "Dill first showed promise as an entrepreneur... In 1864, Governor Thomas C. Fletcher, a man given to unusual actions, decided to hold his Inaugural Ball in Fishers Cave...

"When Dill took over, this bit of history had been all but forgotten, and the dance floor had rotted away. But one Sunday a visitor spotted a handmade, square nail from the old dance floor. Word got back to a St. Louis reporter who dug up the story of a ball (which, according to newspaper accounts of that day, should have been called Inaugural brawl) and the result was a big Sunday feature story.

"People flocked to the cave to look for square nails. Business was great until there were no more square nails to be found. But the hills in the area were covered with falling-down corn cribs and out-buildings that had been built with square nails. Dill sent out word that he would pay a dollar a gallon for square nails. Times were hard. The buildings went down and the nails came in.

"Every Saturday night Dill would salt the cave with a few dozen nails. Then one day an experienced reporter came out, looked him in the eye, and asked, 'How come you never run out of square nails?'"

"Dill prides himself on the fact he has never told a deliberate falsehood to a

steps, upward into a large passage where the tourist route trends west along an avenue 10-15 feet high and 50-60 feet wide. The passage floor is largely of clay. It has been deeply incised by the cave stream. Bridges span the muddy clay gulleys.

Along this route visitors can examine numerous "bear beds", the old "cemetery", "old ivory", "Santa Claus's Chimney", and the "petrified forest", the latter being a veritable jungle of speleothems composed largely of stalagmites, stalactites and columns.

At a distance of 1500 feet from the cave entrance the commercial trail enters the "Ballroom", one of the cave's greatest chambers. Speleothems abound in this room. Wall dripstone is plentiful. Stalactite-draperies hang from the ceiling in clusters of giant stone curtains.

From the "Ballroom" the cave leads in two different directions. The left hand fork, known as the "Weeping Willow Passage", has approximately 1500 feet of surveyed length, some of it only recently discovered. Its terminal point is the famed "Hugh Dill Room".

The right hand fork leading from the "Ballroom", provides access to several extensive arms of the cave, adding approximately 2500 feet of passage to the cave's newspaperman, so he knew the game was up."‡

An old adage says that "necessity is the mother of invention." Les Dill had invented at least one way to temporarily circumvent the state's strict rules about advertising.

"The cave couldn't be advertised like it should be because the state wouldn't give anyone a long term lease on it. It was just one year at a time. You couldn't afford to lease that cave for just one year and spend a lot of money on advertising," says Eddie Miller, a Missouri caveman who worked at Fisher's Cave in the early days.‡‡

The fact that Les had no surplus funds for advertising was another factor.

And so Les looked for other ways to promote. Exploration, experimentation and discovery were avenues he sought to use.

One experiment was with radio. "Ray Dill at Fishers Cave, A. L. Drumeller, State Park Photographer, and L. E. Johnson, radio expert at Sullivan, with several others went to Fishers Cave...Sunday and set up a radio in the Ballroom and got clear, distinct reception, entirely free from static or interference of any kind," said a local newspaper. "The Ballroom is one quarter mile from the entrance, a route anything but straight..."‡

With expansion of Park facilities, A. L. Drumeller became Park Superintendent in 1930. Thomas B. Dill remained as general Refuge Keeper. A zoo was planned for the Park--one to house bears, foxes, raccoons, wolves, and other animals native to the State of Missouri.‡‡

Les Dill had managed to renew his Fisher's Cave concession for a third straight year. In June, while doing excavation near the mouth of the cave, a human skeleton was uncovered. The skeleton proved to be that of an Indian child about 10 years of age. Les saw that this event was brought to the attention of a reporter.

"The bones," the newsman wrote, "were badly decayed but some were enough preserved that the skull, jawbone and ribs could be identified. The bones were found about 20 feet inside from the entrance to the cave and about 18 inches below the surface."✱

Exploration of the cave continued. Figures given by news reporters were often exaggerated, but this created greater mystery, excitement and incentive for visitation.

"...Seven miles of tunnels in new cavern and these will augment the three miles of explored tunnels in Fishers (Cave)," a news account read in August of 1931.✱✱

"Leonard Dill of Sullivan is the discoveror of the cavern being opened. Last winter he found a narrow passageway from Fishers Cave into a cavern by diving under a water-covered ledge about one half mile back in the cave. Later he was accompanied on the hazardous trip by another Sullivan youth..."+

In August of 1932 the local paper reported another new find. "A new discovery in Fishers Cave is a continuation of a discovery made two years ago; is named the Crystal Room. After leaving the Crystal Room, Ray Dill, George Cowan and Joe Noskay, guides at Fishers Cave, on climbing 14 feet up a particular wall found an air crevice at the top. The crevice ranges from 10 to 18 inches in width and from 10 to 50 feet in depth. One quarter of a mile in length, in places the crevice was so narrow it was necessary to break off projecting rocks to get through. Gradually the opening increased into large rooms, some being 50 to 60 feet high. The trip was near a mile in length, and the time required to make the trip was 5 hours. At the end of the cavern is a room 50 feet high with a dome-shaped tower tapering to a sharp point at the top. At this place

Early photograph in Mushroom Cave.
(Photo by Russell T. Neville)

63

was a breakdown with large boulders wedged in as if ready to fall. Tree roots are growing down through the loose boulders at this point, (and) it is certainly almost through to the surface as there was splendid air coming through the opening."++

Fortunately for Les Dill, his well-known, well-loved and colorful father became the subject of more than one reporters news feature. Townsend Godsey, Director of Public Information for the Missouri Game and Fish Department was the author of one article titled "Meramec Park--Missouri's Caveland." In this feature for *Missouri Magazine* he praised Thomas B. Dill in this manner:

"T. B. Dill, who with his sons each year conducts hundreds of groups of persons through the caves, has lived nearly half a century within the Park and knows every stalactite and stalagmite of any size or beauty in the caves. His famous hunting and fishing and wildlife tales have earned for him the title of "yarn spinner." He yet possesses a pipe presented to him several years ago for having told a big yarn, although at the time of presentation he was instructed to present the pipe to any man who could spin a bigger yarn than that one of his.

"Throughout the year this man lives close to Nature..."ɸ

Scenic View in Fishers Cave
(photo by Weaver)

Musically inclined, the Dill boys made the acquaintance of Bryan Berti during the summer of 1931. Berti was county and district singing champion. Les Dill immediately offered Berti a job as a guide at Fisher's Cave, certain that Berti's singing fame could be put to good promotional use. Sure enough, it quickly resulted in news features.

"Bryan Berti...is now working in that cave (Fishers) as a guide and furnishes some novel underground entertainment for the explorer. Berti and the other guides at the cave also play tunes upon the Ballroom's great stalactites known as the rock organ..."ɸɸ

Les took note of this interesting innovation of Berti's. He would have a use for it again someday.

Les Dill's next ploy was to get Bryan Berti featured on radio. In July of 1931 the local paper reported "Bryan Berti... and Dill family fiddlers, all of Meramec State Park (were) featured in a Meramec State Park hour over radio station WOS at 7:30 p.m. July 15...(The) Dill brothers (are) considered Franklin County's premier fiddlers and guides at the Park's caves..."‡

Through the efforts of the Dill family, Meramec State Park grew and prospered as a "Playground" for the peoples of St. Louis. Fisher's Cave did especially well. There were weekends when as many as 1,000 people would tour the cave. This was remarkable for the Great Depression was beginning to take hold. Millions of people were unemployed. Before the end of 1933 the Civilian Conservation Corps (CCC) would be organized as part of President Franklin D. Rosevelt's "New Deal" program. And a CCC camp would be established at Meramec State Park. Eventually, the Park would benefit considerably from projects carried out by these youthful government workers.

Les Dill, however, had new worries. He had succeeded in renewing his cave concession for five consecutive years. But politics had changed in Jefferson City. In 1932 the Depression brought about a Democratic landslide. Les Dill's supporters were swept out of office. The new brooms wanted a clean sweep. If Dill wished to remain in the cave business, he would have to look elsewhere. The Fisher's Cave concession would go to someone new just when he had marshalled it into a truly profitable achievement. He would not reap the rewards.

The epilogue to Les Dill's efforts at Fisher's Cave and Meramec State Park were detailed in a news story released in the spring of 1933:

"(A) new highway takes visitors to Fishers Cave near Bear Den Zoo, campground and other attractions. Missouri's popular playground, Meramec State Park in Franklin County is now more inviting than ever before since the opening of the new seven mile scenic highway in the park. More than 1,000 persons have visited the park each Sunday since April 1st. Spring visitors to Meramec State Park are agreeably surprised at the improvements recently made. Included in the development, in addition to the seven mile scenic highway are the establishment of a zoo and the opening of a new campground.

"A recently discovered new wing of Fishers Cave is to be opened to the public sometime this year. The new all weather scenic highway, completed last fall, extends from Elm Spring near the entrance of the park over the ridge above the caves to the east of Fishers Cave not far from the Meramec River. This road, at one point on a ridge peak, circles a great natural amphitheatre which in reality is a sink caused by the collapse of the roof of Bear Cave, one of the largest and least explored caves in the park. While excavating the road on the hill above Fishers Cave a vein of lead ore of good quality was discovered. The famous Hamilton lead furnaces were operated not far from this place and the hills throughout the park occasionally yield specimens of this ore-- (which) have been put on display at the concession now operated at the entrance to Fishers Cave.

"Tourists who have formerly visited Fishers Cave will hardly recognize it, so much has been done toward cleaning up the cavern. A rustic entranceway has been constructed and the cavern floor has been graveled. One may now walk back into the depths of this cave to the Ballroom without soiling ones shoes, as the guides have been active in gravelling the underground trail and rebuilding the plank walk. Recently a couple of boys were employed to carry gravel by the bucket full into the cave for this work. If the cave visitors desire to go into the cave without having their shoes slightly soiled, overshoes may be procured from the guides. Equipment carried by the guides includes lanterns capable of providing illumination sufficiently powerful to penetrate the darkness in all the rooms and passages.

"Virtually all the rooms in the cavern except those only recently discovered are visited on each guide conducted trip made into Fishers Cave.

"The new section which will perhaps be opened this season is said by the sons of T. B. Dill, game Refuge Keeper, whose family has explored all the known caves in the Park, to be larger and more beautiful than any other cavern in the Park. A heavy charge of flashlight powder set off in one of the rooms in the new wing failed to make enough light to penetrate the depths. In discovering the new wing, Raymond Dill, a son of the game Refuge Keeper, crawled under a narrow ledge of rock in Fishers Cave for 100 feet. This new wing is believed to be a part of Bear Den Cave, the entrance of which, is more than a mile from the entrance of Fishers Cave. The Scenic Highway connects Fishers Cave with the best campground, the Bear Den Cave, and the Zoo. This cave near Campers Spring was formerly known as Sheep's Cave and has now been converted into a bear den. Four Missouri black bears are kept there now."‡

Les Dill would be moving on but not his father. Thomas Benton Dill would remain as Refuge Keeper, aging but still a teller of tales. His wildlife yarns would live on for a time yet, thrilling park visitors, adults and children alike.

Scenic View in Fishers Cave
(Photo by Weaver)

(Courtesy-Halliday, photo by Neville)

Early view of the Parking Lot.

The Great Depression of the 1930's was a time of despair. It was a time of hunger--hunger for food, clothing, housing and jobs. The Nation was in the grip of near economic collapse. And in the face of this bleak situation, Les Dill chose to invest everything he owned to develop a commercial cave. What utter folly it seemed to everyone but him.

Even as he searched for a cave in 1932, banks were closing their doors all across the country. The Nation's business began to grind to a stop. Millions of people lost their jobs, their homes, their health, and their life savings.

"I knew that by 1933 my contract with the State would expire," Les says, "and I'd have to find a cave I could develop if I was going to stay in the business."*

The Meramec River Basin is one of the most cavernous valleys in America. This made Les Dill's task of choosing a cave even more difficult. He hunted for a cave that had size, beauty, outside grounds suitable for future development, and a good location.

To the south of Meramec State Park near Leasburg were three thriving commercial caves--Onondaga, Missouri and Cathedral. Les had watched, with concern and interest, as one cave system was divided up by different land owners. Onondaga Cave was handsomely beautiful and extensive. It ran beneath several property owners. Now the one cave was two cave operations. One segment of the cave was shown as Onondaga, and another segment as Missouri Caverns. The two cave operators were embroiled in a bitter contest for ownership of the entire cave system, and the tourist dollar. Their battle had carried them to the Supreme Court of Missouri. The suit promised to bring both cave operators to financial ruin.**

South was certainly one direction in which Les had no desire to turn. So he gave his attention to caves along the northern boundary of the State Park. This area was not only closer to the family farm but closer to St. Louis. And, to assure himself that he could not do better elsewhere, Les examined caves throughout the United States.

"I toured the country looking at a lot of other caves" he recalls. "I explored the field. I had already been in most of the caves up and down the Meramec River Valley. I finally decided the best was Saltpeter Cave just down the river a few miles from Fisher's Cave."+

The entrance to Saltpeter Cave lay just outside the northern boundary of Meramec State Park. Its huge entrance opened within a stones throw of the river, and an old wagon road, badly damaged by spring floods, pieced its way alongside the river bluffs to the cave mouth. The road began at Stanton, three

67

Early photograph of the entrance to Meramec Caverns

miles to the north. About one mile north of the cave, the road descended from the upland plateau into the river valley where county and state maintenance ended abruptly. At one time the old wagon road had continued upriver along the west bank to the cave, but the river had eaten away at its bank. The road had become hardly more than a foot path and even that was treacherous. "It was just a path and so narrow you'd almost slip off in the river," says Bob Shatz, a native of the Stanton area.++

To avoid difficulties, people had grown used to crossing the river where maintenance ended at what was known as "Sand Ford". Bob Shatz, who played along the river banks in his youth during the early part of the 1900's, says "Down where the state road ends there was a river crossing. They'd cross there to the other side, go upstream until they got to the cave where there was another "riffle" in the river, and they'd cross there."¢

Always the visionary, Les could see possibilities. If he had any reservations, he didn't voice them. Mary Dill on the other hand, was skeptical. "When we first went down there," she says, "there was just a little old wagon track leading up to the cave. I wondered if we had been foolish in thinking we could open the cave."¢¢

Having finally made his decision, Les faced the next obstacle -- Charley Rueppele, the cave's owner.

*   *   *

Charley (C.A.) Rueppele acquired Saltpeter Cave in the 1890's from Joseph Schmuke who had owned the cave for a brief period. While Schmuke and others sought to exploit the cave in some fashion, Charley had other interests. He was a miner by trade and spent much of his time prospecting for copper in the cave's vicinity.

Considered handsome in his youth, Charley lost the use of his left eye at an early age. For the remainder of his life he was self conscious about this handicap. He generally avoided having his picture taken in such a way as to fully reveal his bad eye. It is possible this disfigurement also added to his shyness around women. For whatever reason, Charley never married.

Charley lived with a sister who was also unmarried. Together, they occupied a large farmhouse south of Stanton where they were surrounded by hundreds of acres of Rueppele real estate. Bob Shatz, who knew Charley fairly well, says "He had two sisters that were old maids. His house was so large you could drive into the basement with a team and wagon and turn around. His parents built the house. They also had a vineyard over there and made lots of wine.

"Mr Grandad came from Germany and he worked for Charley's father in the vineyards."‡

After the death of C. A. Rueppele, Charley's father, Minnie took charge of the vineyards, and the wine making enterprise her father had so meticulously built up. As for Charley, his only interest in wine was consumption.

The Rueppeles lived well for many decades following the death of C. A. Rueppele. The vineyards prospered but Charley was not the business man his father had been. His real estate transactions soon began to slip. For a time, however, he did do fairly well at prospecting, making several good strikes in copper and iron. For some unknown reason, Charley found he could not parley his strikes into greater accumulations of wealth. By 1925 his property holdings had declined in value to little more than $7,000.‡‡

Charley was large and muscular in his prime. In the words of Bob Shatz-- "A big, tall man that weighed about 225 pounds."‡ But he began to lose his health at a reasonably early age. And, as his health failed, he began to drink heavily. As one Stanton resident said "Charley would spend all day at the saloon. He spent a lot of money there."‡‡ Until just shortly before his death, Charley was unaware he was suffering from an incurable disease -- cancer. But even before he learned the truth, he suspected something was terribly wrong inside his husky frame.

Local people were used to seeing Charley, very dapper in his dress, an umbrella or fashionable cane on his arm, strolling about town as if he owned the entire world.* He nearly always wore nicely polished shoes, a suit, and a tie. When he began to drown his financial difficulties and health problems in alcohol, some residents spoke of him as "that old drunk." Yet, one Stanton lady who knew him well, says "Charley was actually a pretty good ole boy. He helped people quite a bit around Stanton."**

As the Great Depression swept across the countryside in the early 1930's, "old Charley" poked around even more earnestly in the vicinity of Saltpeter Cave hoping to make a rich mineral strike. He even poked about inside the cave and was thus engaged when Les Dill first approached him about obtaining the cave.

Charley Rueppele had no real inkling of the value of the cave he owned. If anyone had suggested he commercialize it he would have probably pointed a finger at the past. Gideon, Schmuke, Door and even a two-bit hustler had tried to exploit the cave--all to no lasting success. When Les Dill walked up to him and broached the subject of leasing or purchasing the cave, Charley was astonished. Fixing Les with his one good eye, Charley stared at him speechless for a few moments before he even acknowledged Les's query.

Charley was in almost constant pain by this late date because the cancer was located in his throat and mouth. It sometimes rattled his thinking but on this occasion he managed to summon up a little of his father's shrewdness. He reasoned that if caveman Les Dill was foolish enough to think he could develop Saltpeter Cave into a profitable tourist attraction, then he, Charley, would try to make it worthwhile for the Rueppeles. Charley then proposed what he thought was both a reasonable, yet profitable deal. The reasonableness of his offer was something Les wasn't too sure about. For depression years, Charley's asking price was mighty stiff.

"Old Charley had used the cave only for prospecting," says Dill. "The cave was used up as far as mining was concerned. I decided to try to buy it from him on an installment plan."+

CHARLEY RUEPPELE in later life.
(Courtesy- Washington, Mo. Public Library)

Charley's asking purchase price was $20,000. If Dill wanted the cave, he would have to produce $5,000 cash for a down payment, the remainder "to be paid in ten equal annual installments of $1,500 each..."++

Dill was momentarily stunned. The old prospector was driving a hard bargain.

"My whole fortune consisted of $4,000," Les recalls. "The Depression was on and about that time one of the banks (Grand National) where I'd deposited part of my savings, became insolvent. As a consequence, I lost $1,000 overnight. The remainder of my fortune was $2,000 cold cash I had buried in a tin can.

"We were all desperate in our own way. Charley was hurting for money too, so I had heard."φ

Charley was adament for awhile. The next move was up to Les Dill. So Les went looking for a partner and found Edward Schuler. "He said he'd put up $5,000," Les says "and then found he couldn't. But he wanted to stay in the cave deal with me."φφ

A cousin of Ed Schuler, asked about this incident, said "Ed borrowed $500 to go into that deal with Les Dill."‡

After coming to an agreement upon how to approach Charley Rueppele, Les and Ed looked the old miner up. They had a new offer. This time Charley was agreeable.

On May 1, 1933 a lease with option of purchase was finally negotiated with Charley Rueppele and his sister Nina Mack. Ed and Les found themselves with a cave to develop for which they would have to pay rental of $750 per year for a term of five years. By some means still unknown, they would have to exercise the expensive option of purchase within five years or lose everything. The lease had no renewal clause.‡‡

It did not take long for word to get around in the small communities of Stanton and Sullivan. People had mixed feelings. There were some who said that Les Dill not only had a hole to develop, but a hole in his head as well.

"Ed Schuler was with me about a year," Les relates. "Times were hard. We didn't have any money to hire help, let alone do a lot of development at the cave. But I did have friends who were willing to help out when they had some free time. They often doubled as workers and guides. I also moved my whole family down to the cave."Ŧ

CONCESSION STAND
The first Concession Stand was constructed to the   (Courtesy-
right of the cave entrance near La Jolla Spring.   Meramec Caverns)

Among friends who assisted were Bob Shatz and an uncle to Bob's wife. One of the first big chores was to make a passable road up to the mouth of the cave, and to create a satisfactory parking lot.

"There was a big slough where the spring stream came out to the river," Bob Shatz remembers. "I took my sawmill crew down there several times. We'd cut timber. Les would have a dragline and we'd use it to pull the gravel so we could push the river over."‡‡

Says his wife, "You can't imagine what it used to be like when you see it now."*

Since there was very little time between the signing of the agreement and opening day, Les had to forego the creation of a large parking lot to start. He simply graded his road into the mouth of the cave. There was room inside for at least 200 or 300 cars if they were parked right. He figured it would not only be a novel parking lot, but an air-conditioned one at that. Then it came to him. He had the World's Only "Drive-in Cave"! What a unique way to promote his new wonder!

The Concession Stand was just a small wooden structure built low and to the left of the cave entrance as you faced the river. It was so low, in fact, that even the smallest rise above flood stage in the

river would flood the stand.

For the children it was both work and adventure. Betty Pruett, one of Les Dill's daughters, was then eleven years old and she still cherishes memories of that period. This was the same little girl who, at the age of six, ran away from the babysitter so she could be with her parents at the cave--only at the time, her parents were operating Fisher's Cave in Meramec State Park.**

Even at the age of eleven, however, Betty was expected to do a few chores. "The first thing I did," she says "was tie on bumper signs. Part of the time I'd play. One thing I enjoyed was picking up all the burnt matches the guides would throw down from lighting the lanterns. They had a big wooden table in the cave entrance where the lanterns were lined up. So when I wasn't working I'd play with the match sticks making things.

"My sister Francena was older and of course, had more responsibilities."

"Bumper signs", better known today as "bumper stickers" because of their adhesive backing, were rectangular, white cardboard signs advertising the name of the cave. Taylor-made to fit an automobile front or back bumper, they were wired to car bumpers by cave guides while the visitor was on a cave tour. Although a means

TWO EARLY GUIDES
A modern day Gift Shop now occupies the spot where these two early day guides stand. Note sign saying "Do Not Molest Nature". (Courtesy- Bob Hudson)

71

JESSE JAMES CORRAL
Early day visitors could also take trailrides
along nature paths in La Jolla Natural Park.

(Courtesy-
Meramec Caverns)

of obtaining free publicity for however long they stayed on the car, the signs were originally considered "souvenirs" and travelers of the first half of the 20th century often displayed them with pride. They were sought after treasures of a happy vacation.

Les Dill was the first caveman to use this form of advertising. He concocted his first bumper stickers in 1928 while operating Fisher's Cave. The experiment proved so successful he has continued to use "bumper signs" ever since.

Having renamed his new attraction Meramec Caverns, Les Dill opened on Decoration Day 1933.

"We charged 40¢ per person and had six people on our first day," Les recalls. "There were no steps up to the Wine Table Room. We just had a rope people used to pull themselves up the incline by... We didn't have but one outhouse and it was used for the womens' "john". The men had to use a big hollow Sycamore tree!"+

Les, Ed, family and friends, rebuilt the deteriorating old dance floor inside the cave's spacious "Ballroom". Dances seemed to be a promising way to obtain publicity as well as boost profits.

Dances quickly became the bread and butter of the infant cave operation. The Depression had badly depleted tourist traffic. There was very little highway traffic to draw upon, and yet, "on July 4, 1933, we had 332 people" Les remembers.++

There was even a welcome feature in the local paper although the reporter seemed unsure of the lasting qualities of the cave's new name. Titling his article "Lester Dill Operating New Cave Resort", he wrote "Salt-petre Cave open to public for the first time under new name. Several Sullivan people have attended dances held recently on the new dance floor built in the Meramec Caverns... Salt Petre Cave is the only cave in Missouri in which dancing is arranged and one may dance very comfortably there as the temperature is 65 degrees at all times... A new road has been built from the Sand Ford to the cave and a parking space has been provided for within the cave for 150 cars...

"Four thousand feet of lumber has been used in making stairways to the different levels.

"There are many unique formations in the cave, among them being the "Cathedral Tower", "Wine Room" and the "Natural Stage". Mr. Dill expects to complete an electric lighting system throughout the cave soon. These as well as many other picturesque formations will be beautifully illuminated.

"The large spring near the entrance.. ..has been named La Jolla Springs.."¢

Les Dill had a cave of his own at last. He was off and running but the race had only begun. The coming years would bring greater success--but they would also bring despair and tragedy.

MERAMEC CAVERNS ENTRANCE
This view was taken in 1939, just after the installation of
electricity, and shows the World's First Drive-In Cave.

(Courtesy-
Meramec Caverns)

MERAMEC CAVERNS OFFICIAL CAR
Les Dill, in official attire, stands beside
his car in the entrance to Meramec Caverns.

(Courtesy-
Meramec Caverns)

WORLD'S FIRST DRIVE-IN CAVE
Three early day automobiles park in the cool shade
afforded by the large entrance to Meramec Caverns.   (Courtesy-Halliday
Note large boulders just outside the cave entrance.   Photo by Neville)

KEEPING COOL
A visitor's car keeps cool while its owner tours Meramec
Caverns. A competitor's bumper strip shows plainly. (Halliday-Neville)

CAVE ENTRANCE, EARLY 1940'S
Meramec Caverns Staff gather for a group picture.

The World's Only Drive-in Cave. No native Ozarkian had ever heard of such a thing. It was a novel way to promote a cave. There were Depression day St. Louisians, traveling with only a few dollars in their pockets, who made the 60 mile one-way trip to the cave just to find out what a "Drive-in Cave" was. They didn't always go through on tour however.

Robert (Bob) Hudson, an early day guide, recalls that selling tickets during the lean Depression years was not easy. Each potential customer was coaxed and encouraged. Guides, hustling for ticket sales, invented ingenious ways to develop a sale. And it was a guide's responsibility to see that every visitor was approached as soon as he set foot on the premises. In those days a ticket seller was called "a pusher", a term that has fallen on evil meanings in this day and time. It is no longer a part of caveman lingo.

And when a customer went to pay, he often had to empty his pockets to find enough nickles and dimes to cover the small admission charge. It was not unusual for a visitor to pay for his ticket in pennies.

Eddie Miller, another early day tour guide, remembers parking cars inside the cave. "We'd get cars jammed up inside that cave," he recalls. "Sometimes it was a mess. Les, of course, always wanted a few employee cars parked inside the entrance just for publicity because they called it a "Drive-in Cave" and he wanted us to live up to the promotion claims.

"In hot weather people would park their cars in the cave with windows rolled down. When they left, they'd roll their windows up and fly off taking that cool air with them. No one had air-conditioned cars in those days. But for a few miles they were as cool as cucumbers."*

Among the friends who assisted Les from time to time, was Vivian (Pete) Peterson. A well-driller by trade, Pete was a big, slow, cigar-chomping, easy-going, easy-spending fellow who liked caves. He was enthusiastic over Les Dill's new enterprise. He was happy for Les, since they were old high school chums. But Pete also flirted with the idea of becoming a partner. Before the second season was under way, Les had sold Pete half-interest in the cave for $200. Pete also bought out Ed Schuler for $400, paying $25 down.**

"I had known Pete for a long time," Les says. "It was a funny thing, but we really met on a sleigh ride. For awhile there after Pete bought in we thought we were still on one."+

Pete, reflecting upon those early days said, in 1947, "We started...with a pocketful of nothing, but with heads full of dreams. That first year we took in only $700 and we put it all back into improvements."++

PETE PETERSON in Military Uniform
(Courtesy- Bob Hudson)

In April of 1934, on the eve of their second season, Pete and Les found themselves faced with a serious situation. Charley Rueppele's health had taken a turn for the worse. Doctors offered little hope that he would survive the summer. Quartered in a St. Louis hospital, liquid nourishment was now the very best that Charley could consume. Most of his tongue had been removed to ease his suffering.⊕ But it was a losing battle. Death soon claimed him and for Les it was a double tragedy. He had lost a growing friendship with the venerable old prospector and found himself faced with the executors of the Rueppele Estate. They would want a settlement. The option to buy would have to be exercised. Where would he and Pete find the money?

★   ★   ★

Charley Rueppele had been hospitalized in April of 1934. His sister Minnie, with whom he had lived for so many years, had died six years earlier. There was no one close to look after the family interests, so his surviving sister, Nina Mack, from Los Angles, returned to Stanton to temporarily take charge. Following Charley's death, Nina Mack and Herman F. Hansen served as executors of the Estate.

The summer of 1934 was more successful than the summer of 1933 for Meramec Caverns. Les and Pete were convinced they had to purchase the cave. During July and August there were days when as many as 100 people toured the cave. By todays standards that was miniscule income. By Depression standards, it was a fortune; and the Depression was getting worse, not better.

The dances were also prospering and word had spread about the fantastic underground Ballroom. Organizations dickered with Les for use of the dance floor. The American Legion and Odd Fellows were among the first fraternal groups to utilize the facilities.

Les met with Nina Mack to discuss the lease and see how she viewed the matter.

Minnie Rueppele's death in 1928 had brought the near demise of the family wine making enterprise. That had been Minnie's domain. In Charley's care, after her death, it declined. Charley's lack of interest, determination to be a miner, and his failing health, all conspired to ruin the winery. The vineyards grew up in weeds. The grapes rotted on the vine.

Nina Mack, aging though she was, made an effort to reestablish the winery. She owned a good wine press and paid 25¢ a day for labor. After a time the situation improved and things began to look promising. She was willing to let Dill and Peterson exercise the option to purchase the cave but there were two troublesome matters-- Les didn't have enough money to meet the stipulations of the agreement worked out in 1933, and there were family heirs in Germany who were hesitant. Quietly, she offered to loan Les Dill $3,000 so that he could purchase the cave. But Les and Pete hesitated. That was not quite what they had in mind.

"All I could offer was $2,500 for that cavern," Les says. "That was the sum total of my savings and I had enough faith in the old cave to gamble it all, even in the face of the deepening Depression."⊕⊕

Les began trying to borrow money. Bank after bank turned him down. What could he offer for collatoral? A hole in the ground? It was all they could do to avoid laughing in his face and for some, their smiles said enough.

Les went back to Nina Mack. He could not correspond with the heirs in Germany. They spoke no English and were not knowledgeable enough about the situation to discuss it reasonably. Still, he did not want to borrow any money from Nina Mack, and, in her own way, she understood his feelings. So Nina took up the cause and delt with the heirs in Germany. "She was awfully nice to us," Mary Dill recalls, "especially in communicating with those in Germany."‡

The heirs finally accepted. The cave was actually only a small parcel of the Rueppele Estate. There certainly were no other takers and consequently, the Rueppeles had little to lose.

Until now, Dill's lease money had purchased only time. Henceforth, all payments would bring him closer to a clear title.

Having settled with the Rueppele heirs did not mean an end to the financial struggle. With Pete at his side this time Les once again went in search of a loan. And he was better prepared for the scrutinizing questions the bankers might ask.

"We knew we needed some way of telling the people what we had and we decided roadside signs were the best" Pete said in 1947.

"We also knew no banker, the times being what they were, would lend us the money for that purpose. So we told the banker we needed the funds to lay in supplies for the concessions. These would have a ready turnover and would pay out the loan. Instead, we got our signs, designed and constructed them ourselves. Anybody with a $10 bill could have bought out our stock of goods that season."‡‡

Les Dill relates: "A man who sold me soda pop told me that Orange Crush was putting out a lot of highway signs and so was Budweiser. He got me a bunch. Those sign panels were about three feet by six feet. We found that if we put three of them together we could have a pretty good-sized sign, about six feet by nine feet. That's what we did, and then we just painted over them.

"We put up 14 signs in two days. We had a couple of trucks and a crew of men from around here and we worked awfully hard. We had plenty of beer to keep us going. I also had some pints of whiskey. I'd talk to a farmer about putting a sign on his land, and I'd give him a pint of whiskey and some free passes to the caverns and maybe that would be all he'd want for rent. You know, maybe his wife wouldn't allow him to keep whiskey if she knew about it. And we had some boxes of chocolates in case the farm belonged to a widow woman."‡

Up to this point in time Pete Peterson had continued to follow the well-drilling business. But the cave needed closer supervision, so Pete elected to give up his drilling and work the cave full time. Les would still maintain two jobs. He was also employed by the Civilian Conservation Corps. Pete was a bachelor but Les had a family to support. He needed the extra security the CCC job provided.

"I lived in a tent near the river bank for four years," Pete said nearly a decade later. "I spent almost all of my time in the cave. Les was lazy; he only worked about 18 hours a day. He'd get up with the sun, loaf around the cave doing easy chores like mixing and wheeling cement, then hustle off to his real job at the CCC camp. After taking it easy there all day, he'd come back and dally around the cavern half the night."

"Yes," says Dill, "we lived on pork and beans, and not very much pork. Once when we were really desperate for meat, we got a deer, after matching each other to see who'd go out and play Daniel Boone.

"Pete had an old car. It was a sorry jalopy... The trunk was full of tools. It was our machine shop and without it we never would have kept things going and the road open. And without the road, no visitors, and no visitors, no cave."‡‡

Mary Dill, recalling the days when Pete was there, relates "Pete Peterson was a pretty nice fellow. He was a slow going type. He was honest and had a lot of good ideas."*

Eddie Door, an early guide, has memories of Pete also: "Pete was around the cave more than Les was. Pete did most of the bossing. But he never guided. All

Les and Mary Dill beside
first Gift Shop Building
(Courtesy-Mary Dill)

CAVE ENTRANCE AND PARKING LOT
Note many shade trees and heavy foliage that existed
in the parking lot in the early days. (Courtesy-Meramec Caverns)

the guides were boys that came from around
Stanton and Sullivan and Pete treated them
like they was his own kids."**

Eddie Miller, another early guide,
well remembers Pete's "grub". "Pete
brought us supplies. I never ate so many
eggs and so much bacon in my life. Pete
always bought that heavy, thick kind of
bacon."+

Les Dill, recalling both Door and
Miller, remarked "they were the most
starved to death kids I'd ever seen."++

The first guide quarters was a tent.
From the owner down to the lowliest worker, housing in the summer was the same.

The tent grew and changed with the
years. At first, snakes were a problem.
This was eliminated easily enough by making a wooden floor and wooden sides up for
a few feet. Eventually, the tent living
became cabin dwelling. Things were im-
proving.

By this time Les had nearly two dozen

road signs, and had printed his first brochure. He decided to try radio advertising again. His first attempt was in 1927
while at Fisher's Cave.

"We started advertising on radio," he
says. "Two spots between innings of St.
Louis baseball games. That cost me $150 a
week and I had to borrow the money at a
bank in Sullivan. The banker said he
didn't think that was the right way to run
a business. When the weekend rolled around
so many people showed up that they sold
out of gas in Sullivan, sold out of food,
everything. On Monday I went back into
the bank with a roll of bills that would
choke a horse and I told the banker maybe
he should start running his business the
way I was running mine."◊

With this success ringing in his
ears Les Dill had every reason to believe
"that the automobile was here to stay,
that good highways would come, and that
tourism would someday be very big business."◊◊

"The more I worked," Dill says, "the

more I was sure of my idea. And the more faith you have, the surer you are of success."‡

Les and his crew prepared for the 1936 summer season. Among the many chores to be done was repair of the Ballroom dance floor, and improvement of automobile parking facilities both inside and outside the cave.

Like most caves, moisture was a constant problem. "They had wooden stairways in the cave for a long time," Eddie Door says. "The water kept them slick and they had to be wiped off frequently."‡‡The same was true of the Ballroom dance floor.

It occurred to Les that maybe the dance floor could be dried out with a gas torch. "I hired a local plumber to dry up the moisture...and the feed line broke under 40 pounds of gas pressure, throwing a stream of flame right below my knees," Les still recalls vividly.‡‡

Les Dill was badly burned from the knees down. Tragedy had struck again, this time very close to home.

BUMPER STRIP BATTLE
Competitors wage war for space on car bumpers
(Courtesy-Halliday, photo by Neville)

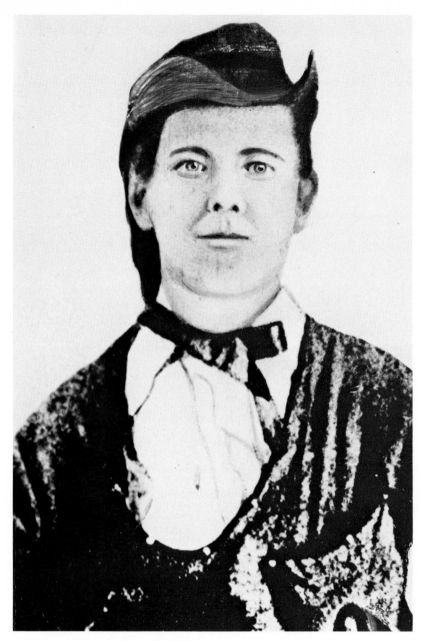

JESSE JAMES AS A YOUNG OUTLAW
(Courtesy-State Historical
Society of Missouri)

JESSE'S SECRET

Johnson

Les Dill was hospitalized for seven months in the Veterans Hospital at Jefferson Barracks. While recuperating from his burns, Les had time to think about his cave problems. He did enough reading on caves to arrive at the conclusion that when commercial caves failed, it was usually because the owners or operators failed to promote and advertise their cave properly.

When Les was back on his feet again he learned that his financial problems were as bad as ever. To survive in business, he would have to borrow again.

The banker's reaction to Dill's request for a third loan was incredulity. He looked Dill straight in the eye and demanded "Why should I give you another loan?"

Dill, nonplussed, met the man's steady gaze and said, "Because, if you don't you'll never get the other two loans back!"

He got the loan.

It was several years before Dill learned why the banker decided as he did. "He told me," Dill says, "that it was my gall, not faith in the cave, that prompted him to grant me the loan."*

Dill threw himself back into the cave work with enthusiasm. His work ethic effected everyone about him, especially his children. "Dad believed we all should work. I was thankful for it," says Betty Pruett.

Les also had firm convictions on how to make his cave even more successful. "If you stand still, my Dad has always believed," says Betty, "your business will go downhill. He thought you ought to improve the cave, the grounds, or something every year."**

Determined that his cave would be open every day of the year, Les stayed with it day and night. In the winter he fought ice and snow that made the hilly road between U.S. Highway 66 (I-44) and the cave, a treacherous route. In the spring he fought the flooding Meramec River which could turn his parking lot into a lake, wash away his souvenir and concession stand, and flood the cave's entrance area to a depth of several feet.

"I fought that river like hell," he says. "I built rock dikes. I dredged the river channel. I changed its course where ever I could. And I finally got things pretty well under control.

"Little by little the improvements got made and my loans were paid off."

By 1936 the United States was beginning to recover from the Great Depression. The national income had risen sharply and industrial production had doubled. However, more than nine million men and women were stil

81

WINE TABLE
This view of the "Wine Table" and chamber shows the graveled
floor. Note absense of formation on floor, which have been
covered by gravel fill for walking convenience. (Halliday-Neville)

unemployed because many factories and mines were still closed or working at less than capacity.

Three million people in 1936 still worked on government relief projects. Even Les Dill still depended heavily on his CCC job for economic survival.

By 1940 it appeared that recovery was complete, yet a new fear hung over the heads of Americans--the possibility of World War. Hitler was on the march across Europe.

As the European war progressed, people became air raid conscious, even in the United States. Dill sensed this and realized that "Meramec Caverns was the safest bombshelter in the United States."+ He began to talk it up and it didn't take long for story-hungry reporters to catch the drift. They came knocking on Dill's door and he was ready for them.

"Meramec Caverns has stood untouched for hundreds of thousands of years," he was quoted as saying. "It is way down in the Ozarks without anything overhead to identify it, and far from a big city. Guess it would be an ideal hideout for any big emergency."++

A Chicago newsman wrote: "10,000 persons can be accommodated in the four floors of the ancient caves which are 250 feet below ground...

"There are fish in the river and wild game within a few hundred feet. A spring bubbles up with 5,000,000 gallons of fresh water daily."∲

In promoting his underground parking lot, Les said that 300 cars could be parked within the cave, and 500 cars outside. Such figures allowed readers' imaginations to play games. The cave sounded huge.

Once visitors arrived, they were not only allowed to park in the cave, but upon purchase of a ticket, received a "Bomb Shelter Pass", useable, it was said, for access to the cave in case of an air raid or other national emergency.

Also stepping up promotion of group and organizational activities in the cave's underground Ballroom, Les offered his naturally air-conditioned amphitheatre for free! Each user, he reasoned, would be a walking advertisement. Once they had partied in the Ballroom, viewed some displays about the cave erected in the entrance corridor, and been duly impressed with the cave's initial size, their curiosity would bring them back later to buy a ticket and see the remainder of the multi-level cavern.

One of the more unusual activities held in the Ballroom was an American Kennel Club Show. On July 12, 1941, the *Chicago Daily News* said:

"In keeping with the idea of letting dogs alone during summer months, the American Kennel Club grants no show licenses in crowded communities. The show licenses issued during the hot weather are confined to summer resorts and country locations. Shows held outdoors are favored.

"Dog fanciers around St. Louis came up with a novel plan this summer when they ferried their coon hounds out to Meramec Caverns and held a bench show in the cool cave...

"Flash Stanley, familiar to those who attend sportsmen shows--for he has staged several indoor coon hunts--was a leading factor in the development of the cavern dog show and he reports the cool temperature was just what the dogs wanted."⊕⊕

Les even went so far as to pull an old rabbit out of his bag of tricks. Remembering the radio stunt at Fisher's Cave in 1928, he invited the same man to try his luck at radio reception in Meramec Caverns. And, of course, it made the papers.

"L.E. Johnson took a new model Zenith portable radio into the Meramec Caverns last Sunday to see what sort of reception he could get" the paper reported. "It had been said that no radio was possible. Mr. Johnson found that the radio worked very well in all the rooms but was of particular clarity in the highest room and in the Wine Room. He picked up a world news report in the high room and an excellent musical program in the Wine Room.

"About ninety people were in the cavern Sunday when Mr. Johnson tuned in his radio..."‡

Dill's blitz of advertising, aimed at promoting Missouri as an ideal vacation state, did not go unnoticed. In July of 1941 the *Watchman Advocate*, a St. Louis newspaper, observed that "The State of Missouri and the Ozarks Region in particular have felt the influence of good advertising and that advertising has been the program of two men who jointly operate one business--Meramec Caverns.

"A checkup of visitors last Sunday revealed that 32 states, Canada, the Canal Zone, and the Hawaiian Island were represented...

"Good advertising brought practically all of them. The treatment the visitor receives is half the merchandise he buys when he goes on a vacation.

RADIO UNDERGROUND
A different approach to the use of radio underground
A radio program is broadcast from the "Ballroom".
(Courtesy-Meramec Caverns)

83

"Lester Dill and Vivian (Pete) Peterson are selling the Ozark Region of Missouri in its entirety every day to their visitors... Dill and Peterson have put into use and demonstrated the old adage, 'whatever helps our business, helps all of us and whatever helps all of us, helps our business.'"‡‡

*   *   *

In his ten years of operating caves, Les had already met many unusual people. Some became close friends. One of the more interesting was Dr. J Harlen Bretz, a geology professor from the University of Chicago. Dr. Bretz was a cave enthusiast and he often came down into Missouri to explore caves.

"I first met Dr. Bretz when he came down to Meramec State Park to see Onyx and Fishers Cave," Dill says. "He found out I knew all about the local caves and asked me to take him around to see them. I kinda liked the ole boy. He never would dispute your word. He'd explain it to you that you were wrong--and he taught me a lot about caves I didn't know."‡

Until 1940, the entrance passage of Meramec Caverns had been thought to generally end at a point 650 feet inside. Here, Les had built stairsteps up to an opening that led to three higher, well decorated levels. Les had long been suspicious,however,of a quiet pool of water that seemed to terminate the first level just a little northwest of the foot of the stairs. So, he invited his friend Dr. Bretz down for a winter weekend of cave exploring. Fifteen years later,Dr. Bretz described what happened on that eventful weekend:

"As late as 1941" he wrote (*Caves of Missouri*, 1956), "this siphon stood full of water to its ceiling, and although the lowest level had been entered by another and very difficult route, no one really knew that a connection was possible here. In December of that year, the writer (Bretz), two graduate students, the owners of the cave (Dill and Peterson), and a few other helpers succeeded in making the first traverse through this water-filled passage. Our plan was simple. We would bail out enough water to make room for a rowboat to pass under that ceiling.

"Across the gentle slope of the earthen floor on the near side of the pool, we dug a trench, made a dam of the excavated earth, and in back of this we emptied the buckets we had dipped full from the pool. After some three hours of this work, with repeated strengthening and raising of the crest of the dam, we lowered the surface of the pool 8 to 10 inches below the wetted ceiling. Then we chopped a rowboat out of the ice along the river's edge (Meramec River outside the cavern

THE KEY TO JESSE'S SECRET
Known as "The Pond", this quiet, unpretentious pool hid Jesse's secret escape route. Photo taken in 1939. (Courtesy Halliday, photo by Neville)

JESSE'S SECRET PASSAGE
"The Pond", drained, revealed this passage to the cave's lowest level.
Modern day visitors travel over concrete trails where Jesse James had
to swim for his life.   (Photo by Johnson)

entrance), dragged it into the cave by automobile, and launched it on our lowered pool. Three of us lay down in the boat bottom, and by pushing with our hands against the ceiling we submerged the boat sufficiently to inch our way under and through. Mr. Dill, remaining behind, wished audibly that the cave could get some newspaper publicity out of this stunt. The suggestion was immediately made that he needed only to break the earthen dike after we were through, and then there would be front page headlines in next day's Chicago papers about one professor and two students of the University of Chicago trapped in his cave; slowly freezing, starving, perhaps drowning. He did not break the dike.

"About 25 feet of this unusual rowboating was necessary. Beyond this distance the ceiling was adequately high, and another earthen floor was found at about the same level as that from which we had launched."‡

Thus it was that the cave's huge, underground "river level" was discovered.

Jesse's secret had been found at last. His escape route would become famous.

In the months to come Les and Pete led exploring parties into the fascinating and enormous new discovery. Since the new passage was lower in elevation than the main entrance level, and was coursed by a subterranean river, it was promptly designated "Level Number One". 'Dill now had a five-level cave for public display and more underground passages than he would ever be able to utilize. But he definitely planned to open up a portion of the new level by spring. Through the winter months following the discovery, he kept a crew of men working furiously to clear rocks, build bridges, fashion trails and install lights. He had visions far exceeding any he had ever had before. Yet, he had not counted on World War II. In December of 1941 the Japanese bombed Pearl Harbor and the United States went to war. War would end the Depression but it would also bring rationing, and rationing would bring tourism to its knees. Without tourists, how could Dill's new wonder hope to survive?

MERAMEC CAVERNS

"The 4-Story Wonder" STANTON, MO.

MISSOURI'S LARGEST *ELECTRIC LIGHTED* CAVE
... World's only drive-in cave. Room for 300 cars.

FIRST BROCHURE
This brochure attempted to inform the public of their
attraction. The cave had just been electrically lit.
It told of only four storys because the fifth had not
been discovered as yet. (Courtesy-Meramec Caverns)

THE ARMY AND THE GUIDES

ARMY CONVOY TO MERAMEC CAVERNS
Note Unit designation on radiator of lead vehicle.
Vehicle 12, Battery A, 113th Field Artillery.
(Courtesy- Meramec Caverns)

I was there the day gas rationing hit," says Eddie Miller. "We were doing a pretty fair business. Then the next day not a soul came down. I think there was seven days there, after rationing hit, that we didn't have one person go through the cave."*

Bob Hudson, now manager of Meramec Caverns, was a guide at the time. He relates: "Les went up to Fort Leonard Wood (about 65 miles south of Stanton) and worked out a deal where the practice convoys would come down to the cave and bivouac in the river bottoms. Les would throw them a dance that night. The next day they'd convoy back."**

Fortunately, for Les, his cave was located halfway between St. Louis and Fort Leonard Wood where thousands of soldiers took their basic training. He not only threw dances for them but established special tour rates for men in uniform. It was a captive audience. But the soldiers meant much more--they represented mothers, fathers, wives, children and sweethearts. These came in droves to visit their men in training and the cave was an ideal place to meet, to picnic, and to tour while they visited.

Late in 1941 a news article said: "During the past year probably every state in the Union has been represented at Meramec Caverns by a man in the uniform of Uncle Sam's Army. The soldiers in training camps in nearby Arkansas and Illinois have paid the highest tribute to one of Missouri's beauty spots by coming in "squads" and "scads" to see the four story wonder cave on the Meramec River near Stanton. And as for those who are stationed in camps in Missouri, well, there has been more than squads and more than scads. There has truly been slews of them. Another reason for the great increase in attendance at the cave this year has been the number of parents and friends who came to visit soldiers and gather in a couple of benefits with one trip..."+

The convoy maneuvers were also mentioned in the press: "Practical army maneuvers "underground" were carried out last Thursday at Meramec Caverns and La Jolla Forest, Missouri, when 1500 officers and men of the 119th Field Artillery from Fort Leonard Wood spent a day and night near the Caverns, Stanton, Missouri, and marched into the maw of the big cave in full battle dress.

"In smaller groups the artillery men went through the entire caverns. Meramec, called the "safest bombshelter" in the world, could house 10,000 persons 200 feet underground in case of emergency. The soldiers studied its space for supplies, for munitions, its water supply with bubbling springs, and its isolated defense "hideouts" where a squad of men, with plenty of ammunition and food could hold off a regiment for weeks.

"The officers of the Ozark Cave Association, Les-

JOHNSON

MERAMEC CAVERNS TURNOFF
Junction of U.S. Highway 66 and County Route W at Stanton.
The building of Interstate I-44 greatly changed this site.
(Courtesy-Meramec Caverns)

CONCESSION STAND EXPANSION
The decision was made to 'house in' the entrance to alleviate the
serious accumulation of ice in winter. (Courtesy-Meramec Caverns)

ROBERT (Bob) HUDSON 1977

GROUP OF EARLY GUIDES
(L-R) Sonny Pruett, Buddy Crockett, Mark Hiller
Carl Lafoon and Bob Hudson. (Courtesy- Hudson)

ter B. Dill and V. H. Peterson, welcome more army and service groups to Meramec Caverns and environs.

"At 4 p.m. the Band gave Sullivan a treat in the way of military music as it paraded through the business district..."

"In the evening the Army officers held a dance for themselves at the caverns. About 30 Sullivan girls were invited guests..." ++

The war had other effects upon Les Dill and his crew at the cavern. "Pete Peterson was 34 years old when the draft came along, so he wasn't drafted," explains Bob Hudson. "But he made up for it. He voluntarily enlisted in the Air Corps ground crew."◊

Guides who were just out of high school, were whisked away by the draft and replacement was a constant hassle. Some would return with injuries. There were a few who never came home again. Several returned uninjured to the cave. One of these was Robert (Bob) Hudson.

For Bob, a St. Louis boy, a career in the cave business began at age thirteen. "My parents and I went to Dallas, Texas, to the Centennial in 1936," he recalls. "Coming back we had a week or more of our vacation time left so we pulled down to

the cave. When my Dad saw the Meramec River, he went fishing. You couldn't even get him interested in the cave. My mother and I went up an toured the caverns. I was absolutely bowled over with it."◊◊

For the remainder of that week, the Hudsons fished, cooked out, relaxed and camped in the wooded bottomland along the river downstream from the cave. Bob, consumed with curiosity, explored the bluffs and cave openings nearby. And he "hung around" Meramec Caverns, watching, learning, getting acquainted with the young fellows who guided. Some were not much older than he.

In those quiet, early days at Meramec Caverns, the strong, fatherly presence of Pete Peterson was a stabilizing factor. Some boys just seemed to "drift in" and find a place at the cave, but then those were lean years on the waning edge of the Depression. Charlie Parks was one such lad that "drifted in."

"When I first met Charlie Parks," Bob Hudson explains, "He was an awfully poor boy. He came down around the cave and Pete just sort of took him under his wing. When Charlie was first down at the cave he was so shy, when they'd call us in to eat, if a girl was eating among us,he'd wait until she left. They finally got him to learn to guide. After he did that for

LYMAN RILEY
Lyman Riley was Les Dill's right-hand man
for many years. During the 1950's Lyman
and Les formed a partnership and purchased
Onondaga Cave. In the 1960's Lyman became a Morman missionary and left the cave
work, selling his interest in Onondaga
to Les Dill. (Courtesy-Bob Hudson)

awhile he was alright."‡

Another individual who arrived unannounced was Lyman Riley. "He came there
riding a bicycle," says Eddie Miller. "He
came in and hung around with the boys and
went on tours with some of them... One
day he said, 'Let me take one.' So they
did.

"Lyman took off with some people and
after an hour and forty minutes another
guide started back with some more people.

"Les Dill had come in. He said
'Where are you going?' The young guide
answered 'To let these people join that
tour?' And Les asked 'Well where is he?'
And the guide replied 'He's in the first
big room.' At that Les replied 'You mean
he's been in there more than an hour, is
still talking, still that close, and nobody had gotten bored and come back out?
Hire that boy!'"‡‡

So it was that Lyman Riley became a
guide. And from a guide position he would
work his way up into the field of cave
management and ownership. Caves would become an important influence in the direction his life would take.

In 1936 Bob Hudson had also arrived
unannounced. After a week of "hanging a-
round" he had no immediate desire to go

GUIDES POSE BEFORE STAGE CURTAIN
(L-R) Eddie and Leo Busch,_____ Sappington, unidentified, Jean James,
John Essman, Jean Riley, Bob Hudson, Mike Door, Jim Rethmeyer, Joe Door.
(Courtesy-Meramec Caverns)

back to the city, but his folks needed to return. "I was so 'hopped up' about the cave," he says, "I got my folks to speak to Mr. Dill about letting me work at the cave for the remainder of the summer."‡

Les Dill's daytime absense (he worked at the CCC camp), his naturally stern mannerisms, and demanding nature, gave him a mysterious, almost imperial status among the guides. He was liked but his presense often made the guides apprehensive.

"After I'd been there about three days, I hadn't yet been introduced to him," says Bob. "I was cleaning lanterns and he walked up and said 'I'm Mr. Dill.' I thought, Oh boy! Now I'm going to get chewed out. But, with a grin, he said, 'I understand you've been working around here. Anybody who works around here we have to put on the payroll.' And he walked away."‡‡

The Hudsons had taken their vacation trip pulling a homemade trailer. They left this trailer, their son, and his dog behind in the cave valley. For Bob, the summer of '36 was an unforgettable adventure. The impressions were indelible. He was determined to devote his life to this "underground calling." And he has. Today, 40 years later, he is still with the cave, now as Manager.

The decade 1933 to 1943 was one of many rich memories for those who worked at Meramec Caverns. Not only have times changed and the commercial cave industry grown up, but people and their concepts of what a cave tour should be, have changed.

"Visitors have changed over the years, and the principal of operating caves has changed," Eddie Miller believes. "In those early days they didn't think so awful much about the beauty of the caves. Oh, they liked the nice formations and all that, but the guides pulled more stunts. We didn't have so many families going through. There were more 'couples' and they were out for a thrill; for an unknown, mysterious, spooky kind of adventure. Cave trips were considered kind of scary.

"And it seems like back then the guides were more unusual. There were some real 'characters' that worked at Meramec Caverns in those days."*

Time and memories have forgotten the names of many who guided at Meramec Caverns during this period, but some individuals left very enduring impressions on visitors and fellow employees alike. In talking with the old time guides certain names come up again and again, such as Charlie Parks, Gene James, Captain Anderson, Gordon Reeves, Jimmy Rethmeyer, Norman Hefty, Joe Door, Eddie Door, Charley

YOUNG BOB HUDSON

Bob Hudson, at age 13, stands beside his parents car in the summer of 1936. His pet dog occupies the driver's seat. Hooked behind is the home-made trailer his parents left to serve as living quarters while working at the cave.   (Courtesy-Bob Hudson)

91

Record, Leo Busch, John Schmuke, 'Sonny' Pruett, Albert Crawl, Bill Lewison, Noel Terry, Lyman Riley, the Cosgrove boys, Carl Lafoon and Buddy Crockett. The list could go on and on.

Eddie Door, age 74 and now living at Virden, Illinois, was born and raised at Stanton. His father, John, was involved with the dances held inside the cave in the late 1890's by D. N. Gideon and Joseph Schmuke. And his brother, Joe, who died in WWII, assisted Les in 1933. "My brother helped Les get that cave open. They sure packed a lot of sand and gravel back into it, let me tell you, buddy," Eddie Door says.**

As a young man, Eddie guided at the cave, and also did maintenance work. His nickname was "Dooney". And his greatest weakness was alcohol, to which he readily admits, even today.

"Buddy," he says, "I got fired several times from Meramec Caverns. It was because of the stuff in one of those little brown jugs.

"Mr. Dill would fire me one day and hire me back the next."+

Les Dill,thinking back to those days, recalls that Eddie Door was "an awfully

EDDIE DOOR, CAVE GUIDE

Meramec Caverns Parking lot
in days gone by. (Hudson)

EDDIE DOOR
The double-jointed showman that kept
his audience in stitches, poses here
in his working clothes. (Hudson)

good worker when he was sober. I liked
Eddie Door.

"We used to stack a lot of Green Tree
Beer (in the cave entrance) between 1934
and 1939. Pete Peterson got it. I told
him it wouldn't sell but Pete said it
would...Eddie drank most of it."++

Eddie's most endearing qualities were
his sense of humor and natural acting a-
bility. Ida Schmuke of Stanton, who has
known Eddie since he was a child, says
"Eddie Door was a clown."φ

Double-jointed knees were Eddie's
saving grace.

Donning a big Mexican sombrero, Eddie
would lead his tour from chamber to chamber. His fertile imagination would people
the cave with rocks and speleothems that
resembled a world of comic characters.

At some point on tour, when his audience was especially attentive, Eddie would
stand before them and complain about his
trousers. His problem, as he explained
it, was that they wanted to ride up on his
legs. As he spoke, he would slowly roll
up his trouser legs to reveal his lean,
hairy, banty-like legs. He would then
continue until the pants legs were well
above his knees.

As if he weren't already comical
looking, he would proceed to say "Now
folks, you don't want to stay in this cave
too long. It'll turn your joints to rubber." Whereupon he would throw his knees
out of joint and stand with them bending
backwards grotesquely.

"I used to tell people that the cave
water running down over my head and shoul-
ders is what caused my legs to bend like
they do," he told this writer,after demon-
strating his strange ability. "I never
told them I was double jointed."φφ

Eddie Miller, speaking of Eddie Door,
says "I've never seen anything like it.
He was the only guy I ever saw who could
bend his legs that way. He could kick his
leg and his knee joint would go backwards.
He was a very comical little guy and he'd
have his audience in stitches."‡

There was a guide that painted pictures on muscle shells and sold them to
tourists. One of his favorite subjects
was the "Meramec Indians". No one, of
course, had ever heard of the tribe except the guide, but his story was very
convincing.

This same individual played "resident
professor and was quite capable of coming
up with professional sounding mumbo jumbo
at a moments notice. His "scientific

SOCRATES
The lovable Black Ladrador Retriever
that once'assisted' on the cave tour.
(Courtesy-Bob Hudson)

93

disertation upon watercress" was a total fabrication but "fooled 'em", so the legend goes. Eddie Miller says he often played "straight man" for this funny character.

To those who sold tickets, there are fond memories of Johnny Landing. He was a diligent worker but had poor eyesight. As Bob Hudson tells it:

"Johnny had a broken wrist watch that he carried in his watch pocket. People would come up and say 'When's the next tour?' Johnny would pull out his watch. It would be upside down. He'd very ceremoniously turn it around. He'd cock this one eye, because he could see better out of it, and say 'It'll be leaving in just a few minutes. Get your tickets over there.'

"He'd put his broken watch away and just start to turn around and someone else would ask 'When's the next tour?' Out

would come the old watch, upside down. Around it would go. He'd cock his good eye again. 'It'll be leaving in just a few minutes. Get your tickets over there.'

"His routine would never change. His reply would never change. And the watch never ran. And he'd do that routine again and again and again in succession. It was very funny to watch."‡‡

But not all the "characters" however, were two-legged. The boys had a mascot--a big black Labrador Retriever--that accompanied them on many tours.

"We called him Socrates" says Bob Hudson. "We would give the dog a flashlight turned on. He'd take it in his mouth and follow the guide. When we'd stop, where ever Socrates' light was pointed, that's what we'd start talking about. More than once we had people convinced the dog was trained as a guide."‡

SOLDIERS AT MERAMEC
This group of soldiers view the newly opened lower river level at Meramec Caverns. It was named Mirror River. (Meramec Caverns.)

JESSE'S LEGACY

"THE BALLROOM"
First called "The Big Room", this early photo of "The Ballroom"
shows the first cluster of lights installed within the cave.

The arched entrance to Meramec Caverns is about 20 feet wide and 50 feet high. It is situated at the base of a high, imposing bluff along the west bank of the Meramec River.

Nearly straight for 150 feet, the entrance corridor easily maintains its width and height for this distance, whereupon it curves to the left and opens into the historic "Ballroom". Actually, the center and largest of three consecutive chambers, the "Ballroom" is the largest room on the cave's "Second Floor".

Formed in dolomite limestone, the cave's rock walls are spongy-looking in appearance, a feature geologists call "spongework". Speleothems are notably absent in this portion of the cavern.

No stream is present along the "Second Floor". Except for a few isolated boulders scattered along the way, it was relatively even-floored, dry and uncluttered even before commercial development.

In the late 1930's electric lights were installed and the "Ballroom" was illuminated by a cluster of lights hanging in its center. The lights were held in place by a steel wire strung tightly across the room's center high enough overhead not to be an obstacle.

No true side passages are present along the course of the "Second Floor" although spongework tubes are long enough or large enough to be mistaken for side passages. Bretz, commenting upon one of these remarkable cavities says "One such pocket has been crawled through with difficulty

for a distance of 45 feet although the two ends in the cave wall are only 15 feet apart."*

Six hundred fifty feet inside, the "Second Floor" terminates in a modest chamber about 20 feet high. Here, along the upper left wall is an opening leading to higher levels.

The opening to these upper floors has been considerably enlarged over the years. When Les Dill first discovered it, it was only body-sized. In 1933 he had it enlarged to accommodate a flight of steps six feet in width. A metal railing divided the flight for the convenience of two-way traffic. Double steel jail-like doors hung at the first constriction, enabling the upper levels to be locked at night against unwanted entry and vandals. Today, with the cave entrance completely housed over by Gift Shop, Restaurant and Administration buildings, a locking gate is no longer needed at this point. The steel gates are gone but so is the twisting upward tunnel through which the upper levels were reached via the long, laborous flight of steps. Extensive quarry work has straightened this passage and the steps have been replaced by a skillfully engineered concrete ramp.

Floor levels "Three", "Four" and "Five" pre-

JOHNSON

95

ENTRANCE TO UPPER LEVELS
This photo shows the long flight of steps that led to the cave's upper levels dur- the early days. The large steel gates were locked at night to protect the cave's formations from vandals. (Meramec Caverns)

sent a variety of beautiful formations, including some of the most highly acclaimed and outstanding underground scenes in America. Even higher levels are known but are too small and inconveniently located for commercial development. And although most of the scenic chambers so far discovered on levels "Three", "Four", and "Five" are open to the public, there are several which have not yet been opened.

Discovering a level lying lower than the entrance passage was an exhilarating event. What had been level "One" became level "Two", or the "Second Floor".

What had been "The Pond" terminating the entrance passage before 1941, became "Lumbago Alley". Drained, its spring-fed water source diverted, the pond basin and siphon became a 50-foot-long passage where tall persons were forced to duck.

"Lumbago Alley" led to a grotto soon dubbed the "Jesse James Room" where relics of the Jesse James era are said to have been found shortly after discovery of the submarine level, or "First Floor". These items were situated alongside an anvil-shaped limestone boulder later called "Loot Rock".

Just beyond the "Jesse James Room" explorers encountered an underground

MODERN ENTRANCE TO UPPER LEVELS
Today visitors no longer find it necessary to climb a long flight of steps. Concrete ramps have replaced them. (Photo by Johnson)

stream which was soon determined to be the source of the La Jolla Spring emerging along the foot of the bluff near the entrance to Meramec Caverns.

Approximately 1000 feet of passage along the course of "Mirror River", as the stream is called today, has been developed for public touring. As Dr. Bretz, who helped discover this section, later commented: "Where we encountered water and much sticky mud in our exploration...concrete walks (have been) laid, and bridges built..."**

In the interests of water control, a dam was constructed along the stream course in the vicinity of the "Jesse James Room". Todays visitors hear the noise of this waterfall, often times an impressive roar. It lends dramatic sound effects to the excitement of the Jesse James story as told by guides at "Loot Rock". A bonus feature of the damming was enhancement of the stream, creating better reflections of the cave ceiling where the lighting has been so arranged.

Features of special interest in this section of the cave include the "Bear Dens", "Lava River" and soda straw stalactites.

Beyond this the cave passage broadens to widths as much as 125 feet. Ceilings

sometimes rise 30 to 40 feet above the visitor.

An enormous side passage is soon encountered. It leads north for an undetermined distance and is called the "Atomic Bomb Shelter". Civil Defense supplies are stored here. Originally, visitors were allowed to enter the first 200 feet of the "Bomb Shelter" passage. The old walkway can still be seen leading off into darkness for lights only penetrate to the first bend in the tunnel.

The terminal point of the commercial route on the "First Floor" is the "Jungle Room". It can be aptly described as an area densely forested with stalactites, stalagmites and columns. The speleothems are superb and are presented amid reflective pools as clear as crystal.

This is hardly the end of the "First Floor" of Meramec Caverns. As one experienced spelunking party, permitted to study this section of the cave in 1959 commented: "Meramec turned out (to be)... more extensive than many of us realized."+

Lying beyond the "Jungle Room", early explorers discovered a series of fascinating natural wonders including a room adorned with stalactiflats, a strangely shaped speleothem of no common occurrence.

LOOT ROCK
It was near this rock that relics of the Jesse James era were found. (L-R) Jean McGee and Albert Crawl. (Meramec)

97

Great, mystifying fissures cross the passage walls and ceiling creating as many questions as they answer.

A flowstone curtain, flanked by beautiful speleothems, appears at one point to close off the great passage entirely--but a small hole penetrates its crystalline mass to lead on upstream.

Although most of the easily accessible portions of this upstream section have been visited by spelunkers, vast unexplored regions are believed to exist beyond a clay blockade that still has explorers at an impasse. The day may come when it will be breached and even greater discoveries are made on the other side.

Another passage of curiosity leads off to the north near the "Jungle Room" and is called "Mud Alley". It has been described as an "array of gigantic domes and calcite-covered canyons". Commercial development of this passage is being considered but as of this writing, it is still a wild, undeveloped realm whose sparkling crystal wonders are still shrouded in the toal darkness of inner earth.

★   ★   ★

Through the winter months of January, February and March of 1941-42, Dill and Peterson kept a crew of men working to get a portion of the underground river section open for public visitation by the spring of 1942. In April, the first press releases appeared revealing the discovery. One St. Louis newspaper carried a double-page spread featuring eight photographs of what visitors could expect to see. The article was titled "Underground River Discovered In Big Cave Near St. Louis."++

Another feature titled "Underground River Found In Ozarks" called it the "Greatest Geographical Discovery Since White Man Came to Missouri..." The article continued:

"Probably the greatest geographical discovery in the Middle West since De Soto crossed the Mississippi River was made recently when Lester Dill and Vivian (Pete) Peterson of Sullivan, Missouri, traveled 11 miles up an unknown and unmapped river (sic). The newly found stream is located wholly underground in a cavern about 58 miles southwest of St. Louis, Missouri, in Franklin County.

"Being curious about the origin of the constant waterflow from an enormous spring that comes out of a limestone cliff near Meramec Caverns, Dill and Peterson began planning an investigation of the course of the water more than three years ago. This year during the dry season, they swam under a rock "door" and entered

ECHO ROOM

BOTRYOIDAL FORMATIONS
These clusters of grape-like crystal formations are outstanding
features at Meramec Caverns. They formed under water.(Meramec)

another cavern through which flowed the unknown river. Up to the present time, they have been unable to fully explore the caverns, but all indications are that the cave may extend beyond the county line and could be many more miles longer than the part already explored.

"The entrance to the cavern in which the river is found has been opened. Walkways and electric lights have been installed. Now as the visitors enter this land of yesterday, they can see a collection of bones that were taken from the ageless clay deposits that make up the river's banks. They see formations that resemble rivers of molten lava, bear beds that may have been used no more than 500 years ago, or perhaps 50,000 years ago. The thundering roar of the river echoes through the canyon-like walls and the water, as clear as glass, reflects the ceiling and the walls until it appears that the Grand Canyon in all its splendor has suddenly moved to Missouri. As the trip along the "river-nobody-knows-how-long" proceeds the visitors pass Indian Mounds, tracks that resemble those of modern elk, more bear beds, and banks of clay more than 70 feet thick. In the pools of water sometimes 15 feet deep, there are blind fish..."

"It is estimated that since the new cavern has been opened, the entire population of the St. Louis Metropolitan Area could be adequately housed and protected during a bomb raid..."⊕

The news stories, however, carried no news of the discovery of any relics beside "Loot Rock". During 1941 Les Dill had uncovered a legend which suggested that Jesse James and his men had once utilized Meramec Caverns as a hideout. The guides began to relate this story on tour. Before long the news was out. "Even impossible stories are now being circulated about the Hero of our boyhood," a reporter penned. "In one two-gun bang-bang story he rides full tilt into a cave whose opening is only about half big enough to accommodate a fair sized rabbit... And speaking of cave entrances brings our story of Jesse to the entrance of Meramec Caverns... Jesse used the cave and with good reason. His little band could really lope through its entrance..."

The reporter continued, finally observing that "probably some of their loot is still in Meramec Caverns--perhaps mouldering there in some rocky recess...

99

Could be that time will bring to light a saddle or a gun...Jesse took inside and left as a souvenir of his visit."◊◊

An announcement of the finding of several old guns, a rusty strongbox, and other relics near "Loot Rock"--artifacts the finders believed to have been left behind by Jesse James and his gang--was not long in coming.

More than one gun reputed to have been used by Jesse James can be seen in Missouri museums, private and otherwise.

The find at Meramec Caverns created no great public furor or awakening in 1942-- but it was indeed a sleeper. It was the eve of the return of Jesse James himself.

The next ten years would bring some dramatic and startling events. A World War was to be fought and won. Tourism would come of age. And Americans would witness a strange saga. Jesse James and his band of outlaws would ride out of the pages of history right onto the stage of world events. Meramec Caverns was destined for fame.

KING SOLOMON'S PILLAR
An array of majestic formations in the vicinity of the underground theatre and Stage Curtains Room. (Meramec)

BOMBS, BALLYHOO AND THE "A" CARD

Wayne and Sybil Shuck on their Honeymoon in Meramec Caverns.
(Courtesy- Meramec)

Although rationing initially had a deadening effect upon tourism during WWII, people eventually began to adjust to circumstances and stir; to find ways to escape the war-time blues.

In July of 1945 an Illinois newspaper announced that Meramec Caverns was near enough that "A" Book holders need not remain at home.

"B" or "C" ration book holders by conservative use of their gasoline, can make an occasional trip to Meramec Caverns," the paper reported.

"Meramec Caverns is the place for the entire family to rest and enjoy a day in the country. There is fishing, boating, swimming, for those who like the river; shady picnic grounds for those who want to 'just relax'; thousands of acres of land 'in the rough' for those who like to hike, explore or collect bugs, leaves or rocks...

"It's within "A" Book driving distance."*

The startling and horrifying detonation of the Atomic Bomb over Japan helped bring the bloody war to an end. It also ushered mankind into the Atomic Age. It likewise created a nation-wide surge of interest in Atomic Bomb Shelters. Again, Meramec Caverns was in the news.

"If we were faced with certain destruction from a hydrogen and atomic bombing here in America," asked Ralph McGill, a syndicated columnist, "what 10 persons would you select to be saved in a specially prepared cavern far beneath the earth's surface where the fiery death would not sear and rage?

"A gentleman with a cave out in the Missouri Ozarks, which he wishes to exploit for publicity and tourist purposes-- and maybe even to lease out to fearful men--has engaged a publicity office in New York which informs me I have been selected as one of several judges to name my choice of the 10 to be preserved to get the country going again--and to work with those who may be saved elsewhere on the earth. It is a publicity stunt, but an intriguing one.

"The first reaction obtained was:

"In addition to me, what nine others are you talking about?

"But the stunt presumes one may not name his family, relatives, friends or associates. They are out. With that understood, one confronts the task. What 10 persons would assure us of having enough know-how, philosophy, intellect, wisdom and so on to rebuild a shattered country nearer to our heart's desire?

"We must also assume that books would be saved. That is why I have always insisted that reading and understanding our own language is the

...ST PLACE IN THE WORLD FROM ATOMIC BO...

(St. Louis Globe-Democrat)

101

most important subject in our schools. If a man or woman can read with understanding there are available books, pamphlets and studies on almost all subjects from which a person--able to read and understand--could learn to do almost anything needed.

"Therefore, I don't think we would need any preachers, priests, or religious leaders. The Book would survive and it is all Christian religion. We would not need any newspapermen, lawyers, real estate dealers, insurance men and so on. (This is a rough proposition) It is necessary, too, I think, to lay down another rule. Some of the selections will of necessity have to be symbolic, in that some of the men important to such a problem would be of advanced age. I would prefer to choose some younger men equally skilled in each field. But, not knowing such, known names must serve as the symbol of what is needed.

"I am quite sure that later on other names will come to me--but it was possible for me to get off to a first start. Certainly, Dr. James B. Conant, President of Harvard, would be one. He has a marvelous grasp of the needs and processes of education. He could build a better system of public and private school education than

Lester B. Dill presents an award to famous animal friend, J. Fred Muggs, June 1954 (Courtesy-Meramec Caverns)

we now possess. He is a teacher. He is one of the great scientists, with physics his field. He also is a thinker. We have too few thinkers.

"Next--without at all seeking to name them in any order of importance, but only as they come to mind--I would put down Dr. Hugh H. Bennett, Chief of the Soil Conservation Service. He, or someone equally skilled, would be necessary to confront the tortured earth. Then I think we should have a man of ideas in creating mechanical tools, engines and so on. I would name Charles F. (Boss) Kettering, the genius of invention and engineering, in Detroit.

Then we would certainly need doctors. I think in this field we would need a man who was experienced in diagnosis and public health. I would put down here Dr. James Paullin, of Atlanta, the distinguished former President of the American Medical Association. He could teach diagnosis, practice and surgery. (Naming him reveals me to be a generous person. He is my severest critic insofar as my waistline is concerned. I would depend on him to develop the Haucks, the Colvins, the Equens, the Bartholomews, the Graves, the McRaes, the Hines Roberts and others here of that quality.)

"My next man would be a man experienced in tool making and production of same, a foreman of some plant. I would assume he would have a background of work in many fields and would have come up from the ranks. My sixth man would be a manager--one able to create new jobs, build plants and supply the necessary managerial skill.

"That's all my specialists. I would then name two young men and two young women, all four of whom would have to be recent--within the last five years--graduates of vocational high schools and who have won health and intelligence awards from their 4-H, Future Farmer and Home Maker organizations. They could already be married or be willing to marry before entering the cave to wait out the chaos and fire on the top side of earth. With them I would send the great books of the world.

"With that sort of setup, always remembering I would substitute younger men for the older ones, if of equal skill, I would bet on these 10 bringing back a better United States than the one we have. I would lean heaviest on the 4-H and Future Farmer champions in health and school grades."**

Ralph McGill's approach was rather serious. Hal Boyle, another columnist of renown, took a more humorous approach because he realized it was a publicity stunt. As he said: "Dill recently asked the Reconstruction Finance Corporation for a million-dollar loan to transform his... cave into an Ozark atom refuge.

"Whether he is really looking for a loan or just more tourists it is hard to say. But he also asked a group of writers to nominate 10 Americans who, in the event of national disaster, should be given top priority as tenants of his modern underground Noah's Ark.

"Picking the fortunate--or unfortunate--ten is quite a parlor game.

"I ended up by picking two lists. Dill himself isn't on either--as who, forced to live in a cave, wants to be dunned by a landlord? I bypassed all politicians, too, to get rid of the tax problem, once and for all.

"My first list is purely selfish: (1) My wife, Frances; (2) Me, (3) Gypsy Rose Lee, (4) Thomas Hart Benton, the artist, (5) Tallullah Bankhead, (6) Burl Ives, the guitar-twanging folk singer, (7) a good bartender, (8) a psychiatrist, (9) Oswald Jacoby, the car expert, and (10) Any two-year-old child.

"With a group like this you could have fun indefinitely..."+

The results of this publicity stunt showed up in ticket sales. And up to that moment, was one of Dill's greatest successes in advertising. A natural born genius at devising gimmicks to promote his interests, Les Dill began devoting much thought and planning to ways in which he could sell his cave even better through the printed word. In 1947 he was quoted as saying "The cave business is peculiar. We have to depend on 95 per cent new business. This means we have to make the most of the attractions we have and add new ones if we can."++

Les Dill wanted to find out exactly what his visitors did want. To accomplish this he devised a questionnaire for them to fill out (voluntarily) after touring the cave. This questionnaire, essentially unchanged now for over 30 years, asks the visitor to name the feature in the cave that impressed him; asks how he thinks Meramec Caverns compares to similar attractions; what improvements they might suggest with regard to the presentation of the cave to the public; what they thought of the guides; and what drew their attention to Meramec Caverns, be it road signs, bumper stickers, news articles, brochures, etc.

Uncountable numbers of these questionnaires have been filled out by visi-

Stooping as he walks through a low-vaulted corridor is Representative Walter W. Whinrey of Lawrence County. Legislators agreed a properly equipped cave is definitely a public attraction. Cave owners reported 300,000 visitors—at $1 a person—have toured it since gasoline rationing ended.

LEGISLATIVE OUTING   OCTOBER 1945
Missouri Lawmakers on Picnic-Study of Meramec Caverns (St. Louis Post-Dispatch)

tors. People touring the caverns are still polled several times each year.

And the results?

"The people like for the guides to talk and be friendly," Les Dill says. "The more hot air you feed them, the better they like it.

"When we put in the first electric lights, they wanted more. And when we added colored lights, they wanted more of that."¢

Public taste, however it might be judged, has therefore been a deciding factor in the development of Meramec Caverns--one of the great secrets of Les Dill's phenomenal success.

By 1948 the stunning popularity of Meramec Caverns was beginning to overshadow neighboring cave operations such as Onondaga Cave near Leasburg, 20 miles to the south. The management of Onondaga, embarrassed by this set of circumstances, and having to answer to his stock holders, hired an out-of-state firm specializing in "testing and teaching corrections" to survey the situation. In doing so, the company sent its own employees posing as both shoppers and tourists to both caves. The results were very perceptive.

"In my opinion," one analyist wrote, "a very thorough selling job has been done by Meramec Caverns on the roadside merchants on Highway 66 (I-44). Most of these say they have not seen Onondaga, but have been to Meramec twice. They say, too, that persons returning from Meramec Caverns praise it highly. This is quite logical, since these persons probably have never seen Onondaga, but go to Meramec on the recommendation of these roadside merchants.

"In view of a remark made by a waitress that she got passes, it is my opinion that the two visits of so many are due entirely to passes given them as part of the selling job on them.

"I believe the best eye-catcher sign is the Onondaga Arrowhead, but few of these are up. Meramec has more highway signs, but they do not seem as attractive as Onondaga's.

"From interviews had with others at the caves and other places, it is my opinion, they visit caves due to curiosity induced first by the highway signs, and after inquiry, by the literature and sales talk given by the highway merchants.

"The bumper strips are very effective and play a decided part in forming the visitor's mind as to which cave they will visit. Several persons at Meramec, passed up Onondaga because they saw so many more Meramec strips and decided it must be the most popular and worthwhile.

"Based on my observations...at least three forms of advertising are necessary. These are: the billboards...word of mouth and printed matter..."¢¢

Another investigator for the testing firm filed an even more intimate, revealing and critical analysis:

"I was previously advised that Dill and Peterson of Meramec Caverns were the 'Carnival type exploiters', so I came to Meramec Caverns expecting lots of ballyhoo and was not disappointed. The alleged two-miles from Highway 66 was more like five miles. The great 'Drive-in Cave' entrance was filled with signs and was not being used as the underground garage described by so many along the highways. Loud speakers showed their magnetic throats at strategic points about the grounds, while a sign at the Cave's entrance announced the time of the next

LOOT ROCK
Famous rock in Meramec Caverns where Jesse and Frank James are said to have divided their loot. (Courtesy-Meramec Caverns.)

SCENIC VIEW NEAR STAGE CURTAINS FORMATION

105

'tour' and stated further that tours were conducted every 45 minutes.

"Cave tickets were for sale in the souvenir shop and we were invited to browse there until time to go in the cave. We spent about 20 minutes looking at over-priced junk. There was counter after counter of the same sort of...goods that is found on the counters of any dime store...

"A regular ticket window was at the end of one counter and to buy admission to the cave, one must follow the approved carnival style and present himself at this ticket window. In a corner near the ticket window is a public address system where a man nattily attired in a forest green uniform, woodsman approved style and aptly marked "Meramec Caverns" on shoulder patches, regularly announced the minutes until the next tour. Between times, he showed some old firearms and explained their being found in the cave, supposedly left there by the "James Boys". Romance! Even before we entered.

"Promptly at 12 noon, a young man similarly dressed presented himself at the door and we followed him and a third uniformed man to the ticket gate inside the cave. When our tickets were collected, this last man went back to the cave entrance while our guide moved, alone, farther into the cave, to stop beside an old log cabin..."‡

The researcher, filing this report, continued to expound upon the way the tour is delivered, called particular attention to the dramatic way in which the guides present the cave to the public. He failed to find beauty where even the most critical disclaimers pause to give credit. For instance, he failed to see the uniqueness of the "Wine Table", the "Echo Room" or even the remarkable "Stage Curtains". He was determined to bias his report. He had been paid to find fault, and supposed faults he expounded upon throughout. In so many words he deplored the "showmanship" of Dill's cave presentation.

And yet, in making recommendations to the Onondaga Cave management as to how that operation might be improved upon, his suggestions were largely a mimic of the "carnival style" of Meramec Caverns which he seemed to deplore.

...and common ...t pages of this native home life.

APRIL 12, 1942

River Discovered in Big Cave Near St. Louis

...age in the Meramec Caverns, 55 miles southwest of St. Louis, caveologists L. B. Dill and ...ted a few months ago, started pumping water out, which enabled them to find where ...eeded to dam it up, and the result is shown in these first pictures of the previously secret chamber, which will be open to the public as soon as the work of installing paths and lights has been completed. Where the underground river originates is a mystery, although it has been noted that three or four hours after a heavy rainfall near Sullivan, Mo., there is a perceptible rise in the cavern stream. Its greatest depth is about 15 feet, while the biggest width thus far discovered is 30 feet. The water, cold and exceptionally clear, is believed to empty into the Meramec River, although just where hasn't been discovered.

Painting of Jesse James
by R.G. Larson
(Courtesy-Missouri
State Capitol Museum)

THE RETURN OF JESSE JAMES

Grave of Jesse James, Kearney, Mo. 1898
(Courtesy- State Historical Society of Mo.)

In the late 1940's Rudy Turilli, Lester Dill's son-in-law, assumed a position at the cave. He was soon to find himself in the midst of a strange drama, for in 1948 two events transpired to trigger a landslide of newsworthy happenings at Meramec Caverns.

Early in 1948, according to Turilli, some visitors to the cave alerted him to something unusual they said was about to take place in Lawton, Oklahoma--a news release that might have some bearing on the history of Meramec Caverns. Without identifying themselves or clarifying their cryptic remarks, they left. Turilli was mystified. For a time he simply dismissed it as a meaningless incident.

Then, early in 1949, a Lawton, Oklahoma newspaper story appeared stating that J. Frank Dalton, a resident of that community, was none other than the infamous Jesse Woodson James. According to Dalton, who was said to be 100 years old, Jesse James had not been shot by Robert Ford in April of 1882. A man, he said, by the name of Charlie Bigelow had been murdered instead. Dalton claimed "that the shooting of Bigelow had been a pre-arranged hoax to enable the real Jesse James to retire from his life as an outlaw."

This story startled Turilli. It interested Les Dill also.

Up to this point in time, 67 years since the supposed death of Jesse James, nearly a dozen individuals had made similar claims. All had been proven hoaxes.

The possibility of Dalton also being a fraud occurred to Dill and Turilli, but, ever on the lookout for ways to obtain publicity, they agreed to check the story out. Dill thereupon sent Rudy Turilli to Oklahoma to pursue the story further.

Certainly the people of Lawton were convinced that J. Frank Dalton was being truthful. "Turilli became convinced he had found the real Jesse James and in time rounded up half a dozen centennarians who claimed to be members of Jesse's gang... All swore the old man was Jesse..."*

With Turilli afield, rounding up documents, sworn affidavits and other "evidence" with which to substantiate Dalton's claim, Dill kept an eye on progress.

"After studying the case for a year, and not keeping his investigation a closely guarded secret... Dill let the news slip out that he was bringing the 100-year-old Jesse..."home" to Meramec Caverns, where he would be well taken care of for the rest of his days...

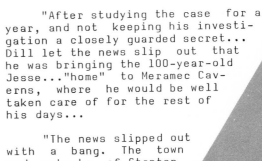

"The news slipped out with a bang. The town and suburbs of Stanton was crawling with reporters. Business at the cave zoomed."**

One feature newswriter, reviewing the story in 1976

(Courtesy-Missouri State
Capitol Museum)

JESSE WOODSON JAMES
Last photo before his death. (Courtesy-
State Historical Society of Missouri)

J. FRANK DALTON
alias Jesse James
(Courtesy-Meramec Caverns)

said "Believable or not, it was a coup in the field of fanfare. That is, it was one thing to say that Jesse James once hid out in the cave and another thing altogether to say you had the real Jesse James in residence."+

Bedridden, due to a broken hip, Dalton was quartered in a guest cottage near the cave and made available to reporters. He was described as being "a lively, white-haired old codger who kept a revolver under his pillow and ordered visitors to 'get the hell out' when he grew tired of their prying questions."

The story broke on January 10, 1950. It was page one news from coast to coast under such beguiling headlines as "Loot Cited As Proof He's The Real Jesse James," "Jesse James Is Bedridden But Still Powerful Actor," and "Jesse (J. Frank Dalton) Says He Has $2 Million In Loot Near Fort Sill."¢

Turilli's evidence was assuring. The "cantankerous old galoot" lodged in the cottage was very persuasive also. Many skeptics left his presence satisfied they had seen and talked with the real outlaw himself.

In 1953, author Phillis Argall wrote "This great array of testimony (by John Trammell, James Davis, John William

Pierce and others), from very old men who had no motive other than to tell the truth as they knew it, comes very near clinching the claim of J. Frank Dalton that he has been, in fact, the true Jesse James.

"In evaluating all this testimony it should be remembered that while these old timers have agreed on countless details of personal experience with Jesse James, none of them had seen each other, nor had an opportunity of talking to each other, for years, prior to their giving their testimonies...

"It is interesting and important to note, also, that in almost every instance when these old men confronted J. Frank Dalton...at Meramec Caverns, or elsewhere, they recalled one or more identifying marks present on Dalton's body and which were known by them to have been possessed by Jesse James. Among them were:

1. A mutilated tip of his left-hand index finger.

2. Evidence of severe burns on his feet.

3. A bullet hole through his left shoulder.

4. A drooping right eye-lid.

5. A bullet scar along his hair line.

6. A scar of a bullet hole in his abdomen.

"While the real Jesse James is widely known to have possessed all of these characteristics and marks,it is only logical to assume that no imposter could possibly be able to exhibit every one of them and did not hesitate to offer them as proof of his real idenity."⧧⧧

Armed with this seemingly irrefutable evidence, the Circuit Court of Franklin County, Missouri, was petitioned to have Dalton's name legally changed back to Jesse James.

While legal formalities were running their course, Dalton was taken to New York for a Broadway press conference. As one reporter later admitted, it "turned out to be one of the durndest whingdings you ever saw."⧧ It also netted wide news coverage, even in the foreign press, which was Dill and Turilli's intention from the beginning. However, what had begun as a publicity stunt was turning out to be one of the strangest historic events of modern times.

Columnist Hal Boyle, confronted by this resurrection of banditry, took his usual humorous approach to reporting the story: "Stay In Your Grave, Jesse James! You're Ruining Old Memories," he headlined his article. But even Boyle was hesitant about denouncing the "old galoot" to be a fraud "Because there is always the odd doubt it might be true", he wrote. He went on to say "And that would be as disturbing as if Robin Hood should come alive again, and lose a bow-and-arrow match with an unemployed Indian."

Boyle acknowledged that many persons were confirmed believers in J. Frank Dalton, but explained that "To the effete east, it is a matter of mere jest whether ole Frank is ole Jesse, but it isn't to anyone who spent his boyhood in the Missouri haunts of the James band. To us Jesse then was a symbol of the defeated south, a man who refused to surrender, who robbed the rich and helped the poor.

"It is a lousy outlaw indeed who doesn't have this robe of glamor thrown around him after death. As a boy we used to search through caves around Kansas City, hopeful of finding some of Jesse's forgotten loot. And it was hard to keep the tears back when we chanted that song about Bob Ford "the dirty little coward, who shot Mr. Howard, and laid poor Jesse in his grave."

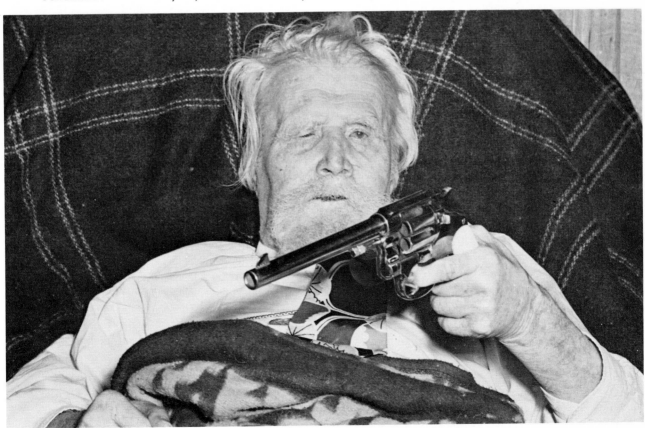

The infamous J. Frank Dalton, alias Jesse James, examines his revolver. (Courtesy-Meramec Caverns)

"Boys are rebels by nature and to us Jesse was the supreme rebel--misunderstood, as all boys feel they are, too, but fighting back. I suppose there are thousands of midwest kids who still hug this legendary Jesse to their hearts.

"This pleasant mildewed memory would be shattered mightily if it turned out that, instead of being murdered by a traitor skunk, ole Jesse had been taking it on the lam from the law for almost 68 years. We want our heroes and our outlaws to die gamely--with their boots on.

"Wouldn't it make you a little sick, even, to hire an elderly paperhanger in a zoot suit 30 years from now and have him turn out to be Adolf Hitler.

"Certain situations in life require certain endings. And the only way J. Frank Dalton could satisfy us he is the real Jesse James is if he were winged and captured by the FBI as he stood, six-guns flaming and beard streaming in the wind, trying to hold up a train to pay off the mortgage on some pore widders shack.

"That was the Jesse we believed in-- although he probably never really lived either. Stay in your grave, Jesse!"‡

Apparently, Circuit Court Judge Ransom A. Breur, who heard the petition to change Dalton's name to Jesse James, either had a different kind of childhood than most boys, or he wisely realized that "truth" in matters such as these, is only a relative thing--never absolute. His judgement of the case resulted in what has been called "one of the most remarkable speeches ever made by a Missouri judge."

"We love Missouri and Missouri's people, but the criminal conduct of what is known as the James gang in Missouri in the past is one thing that has cast a black spot on Missouri...

"For a quarter of a century almost, what is known as the James gang murdered, robbed and burglarized the people of Missouri in defiance of the people, the laws and the courts of this state. Now, after almost three quarters of a century, one who claims to be one of the main leaders of the gang comes into a court of equity-- in the same courts that have been defied-- asking for some relief.

"There is no evidence here to show that this gentleman, if he ever was Jesse James, has ever changed his name. If his name has never been changed from Jesse James, he is still Jesse James in name, and there is nothing for this court to pass on. If he isn't what he professes to be, then he is trying to perpetrate a fraud upon this court.

"If he is Jesse James, as he claims to be, then my suggestion would be that he retreat to his rendezvous and ask the good God above to forgive him so he may pass away in peace when his time comes to go."‡‡

The show was over. Less than 18 months later J. Frank Dalton, alias Jesse Woodson James, passed on to whatever reward was his. We'll never know.

The hearing did not settle the matter legally, of course, but many people remain convinced that Dalton was indeed who he claimed to be. Turilli, thoroughly convinced of Dalton's validity, went on to pursue the matter for the remainder of his life. A few years after Dalton's death, he opened the "Jesse James Museum" at Stanton where the results of his long pursuit still can be seen on public display.

As for Les Dill, he had achieved even greater rewards than he had even conceived from the beginning. Turilli, asked after Dalton's death, "how much publicity the Jesse James episode gained for Meramec Caverns", replied "In inches, I should say that the publicity amounted to the length of the cave."* And that, to say the least, is considerable.

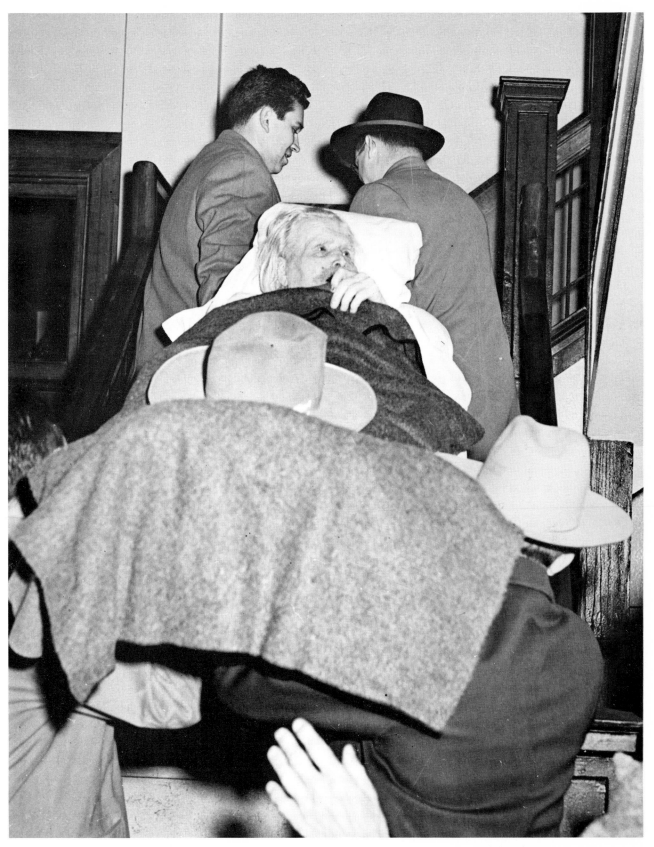

J. Frank Dalton goes to court to get his name changed back to
Jesse James, Franklin County, Mo. (Courtesy-Meramec Caverns)

111

LOVELY MODEL - LOVELY SCENE

112

A PARADE OF
PROMOTIONS

"If it wasn't for Jesse James," Les Dill has been quoted as saying, "my cave would be just another 100,000,000-year-old hole-in-the-ground."*

Well, not quite. Although nine out of ten tourists today say they visit Meramec Caverns because of Jesse James, it cannot be denied that the cave has both size and beauty. And, even before Jesse put in his final appearance in 1950, it was a certified success.

Through the 1950's and early 1960's Les Dill rode the nation's newscolumns to greater heights than ever before. His cave attendance records climbed steadily until by the late 1960's nearly 400,000 people visited Meramec Caverns yearly. Carlsbad Caverns in New Mexico, and Mammoth Cave in Kentucky, both federally operated attractions subsidized by government money, were the only caves in the U.S. with higher attendance records than his.

Dill is not above ribbing a competitor good naturedly and has thrown a few punches at Mammoth Cave and Carlsbad Caverns. As he has said on several occasions "In June, July and August, I do more business than Carlsbad Caverns. That means I do the biggest cave business in the country. But I can't keep up with Carlsbad in the winter so I have to try to build up my winter trade."**

In 1955 one of Dill's thrusts at Texas was replied to by the *Beaumont Enterprise* of Beaumont, Texas. Wrote an irritated Texan: "Lester B. Dill, who operates Meramec Caverns along with a gentleman named Rudy Turilli, and seems to have expert public relations advisers, says he is glad Texans stay away from what he calls his "underground emporium."

"And why does management profess to be pleased because Texas ranks last among the 48 states in state-by-state attendance figures released by the Meramec Caverns... 'Because', says Mr. Dill, 'The few (Texans) who do tour the cave spend more time bragging about the Lone Star State than they do listening to the cave guides.'

"Texans thus disturbing other tourists who, strange as it may seem, are not interested in hearing about Texas but do want to learn something about caves. Maybe there are among them speleologists, described as long-nosed individuals with a penchant for crawling into holes and trying to find out where they lead to, if anywhere.

"So Mr. Dill, talking like a person who is at heart jealous of Texas, declares he is thankful Texans aren't interested in visiting any holes that don't have oil.

"Texans will bear up with their accustomed equanimity under this criticism. Over the years Texas has been criticized by experts but nothing said by outsiders has ever been known to depress a Texan who really loves his

113

Lyman Riley wears the famous "Leopard Spot" jacket on a publicity trip to New York City. (Courtesy-Meramec)

state, as virtually all Texans do with a passionate intensity.

"As for cave-viewing, Texans can get along nicely without seeing the Stanton Missouri hole in the earth that produces no oil but may be a profitable enterprise for those who operate it.

"Texans who wish to go on subterranean sightseeing tours will visit the Carlsbad Caverns in New Mexico, as many do. They think Carlsbad is a better "show" anyway."+

In other news stories Dill likened Mammoth Cave to a big, barren storm drain and said that Carlsbad Caverns was a "dead cave."

The management of Mammoth Cave let the insinuations lie unchallenged but not the management of Carlsbad. Their reply:

"Missouri seems to be doing a pretty good job of publicizing its so-called caves, which are mere gopher holes in comparison with the world famous Carlsbad Caverns. Many tourists, when they reach New Mexico having seen some of the smaller caves in Missouri...think they have seen

"one cave, and one cave is much like another," and thus pass up the opportunity to tour Carlsbad Caverns, little realizing what they are missing, thus depriving themselves of one of the most thrilling experiences of a lifetime. The magnitude, splendor and grandeur of Carlsbad Caverns, surpasses the imagination and cannot be approached by any other known caves.

"Jesse James and his whole gang could have started riding through Carlsbad Caverns, and would not have been through exploring all the passages yet.

"You could dump all Missouri's... gopher holes into one corner of one room in Carlsbad Caverns."++

Les Dill had struck again! As the widely published cave historian Dr. William R. Halliday has quoted Dill as saying, its "all in fun."◊

Almost.

There is still that little matter of "making money". Nevertheless, whoever said you couldn't at least try to have a little fun in the process. Take the New York "Leopard Skin Stunt" for instance.

On a bitter cold day in January of 1954, Les Dill sent Rudy Turilli and Bob Hudson to New York City to "brain storm" with Sy Preston, Dill's public relations link to Broadway.

"We were in New York trying to think up a gimmick," explains Bob Hudson. "The subject of Sir Edmund Hillary came up. He was in town and he had climbed Mt. Everest the year before. Rudy called him on the phone and offered to race him up the steps of the Empire State Building, but Hillary didn't want to participate in such a stunt.

"Rudy decided to go anyway and to see if he could get all the way up to the observation deck dressed in nothing but a Leopard Skin outfit--like a caveman. I went along. He dressed in the leopard skin in a restroom and I held his clothes. He said he was going to tell the guards that he was paying off a bet.

"I left him...When I got back the observation deck was full of policemen and there was a doctor there from Bellevue Hospital. Somebody had pushed the emergency alarm button."◊◊

Turilli had managed to make his way to the 86th floor before he was rushed by policemen.

"We got 10 days in the workhouse," muses Bob Hudson, "and that's exactly where we ended up."‡

LES DILL SAYS "HELLO DOLLY" TO PEARL BAILEY

Dill maintains that it cost him $1,000 to get Turilli and Hudson out of jail but it also netted him reams of sensational newsprint.

For awhile Leopard Skin tuxedo jackets became a trademark with Les Dill. On one occasion he flamboyantly descended upon the City of New York decked out in his latest "leopard" and let it be known he didn't visit the city to admire its tall skyscrapers--he liked the subways better.

New Yorkers loved it. The AP release said "Visitor Shocks New York: He Actually Likes Subways."

As usual, Dill was timely because the subway system was a seamy topic at that moment in time.

"A man turned up here Friday," the paper said, "who says he likes to ride New York's crowded subways. He may be the only one.

"He better be careful about this kind of talk around here, or he might get a ride of another kind--out of town on another kind of rail.

"Denouncing the subway system is the favorite pastime of New Yorkers. They wax violently eloquent by the hour about its jams of people, its breakdowns in hot tunnels...

"Well, it turns out that this fellow who likes the subways is from out of town. And apparently the reason is that he just naturally likes to be moving about underground.

"He's a caveman. Really.

"Not for Lester B. Dill is the Empire State Building, not the Statue of Liberty, the Broadway shows...

'The biggest attractions for me is the subway,' said Dill...

"Dill brought along a leopard skin tuxedo jacket to wear while he and his wife Bess are hitting the town's high spots--or perhaps, in his case, the low ones."‡‡

Once, Dill unknowingly attracted some visitors to his cave he wasn't so sure he wanted to see--the C.I.A.

Dill travels often, and wherever caves exist throughout the world, he is apt to find his way. "One such trip led him, in the late 50's, to caves just outside Havana Cuba. Shortly after his visit, Batista fell to Castro--and when the subject of missle sites arose in 1962, the Central Intelligence Agency (CIA) came calling.

LASSIE VISITS MERAMEC CAVERNS - 1966
(Courtesy-Massie - Missouri Commerce)

"I drew maps of those caves as best I could recall them from memory," Dill says.‡

The same year he met the C.I.A., Les revived an advertising ploy he had parleyed into profits at Fisher's Cave--he promoted a "singing cave guide".

His first, at Fisher's Cave, had been Bryan Berti, a regional singing champion. This time it was Leo Busch, a 30-year-old guitar-plunking native of Stanton. And this time Les had captured a talented fellow who was already known to reporters, who had been featured on television, and who had recorded for Nashville Records.

Dressed "in patent leather shoes, black bow tie and leopard spot jacket", Leo sometimes led tours through the cave and sang popular country music hits. Tunes that went over well at the time included "Hellow Walls" and "Big Bad John".

Teaming up with song writer Ernie Warren, Leo created a song about Meramec Caverns set to the music of the "Missouri Waltz".

"Folks, Route 66 has brought
 you here for you to see,

"The caves where Jesse James
 would hide out all his company.

"For breathtaking beauty and
 excitement and fun,

"The Meramec Caverns are second
 to none.

"Here you'll see a sight that
 takes you back 100 million
 years,

"Built, designed and planned by
 Mother Nature's engineers.

"At Meramec Caverns there's so
 much to see,

"So come along folks, see it
 with me."‡‡

Leo, like a reincarnated Bryan Berti, also took up "rock music" on what he called his "stalagaphone"-- a group of stalactites and stalagmites which give off different tones when struck.

"By striking the right ones I could produce a tune," Leo said. "I worked out the Missouri Waltz that way...

"When I was learning to play the stalactites--I used to do it on my own time to practice, and I worked it up to where I was playing with a stone in each hand.

"Maybe you can't find a sharp or flat you need, but by the time the tone hits the walls a few times--its near enough."*

An even more talented notable than Leo Busch visited the cave--Kate Smith-- who sang "God Bless America" before the "Stage Curtains". At the time, a large group of Missouri legislators were at the cave for a meeting, utilizing the underground "Ballroom" facilities. Kate Smith provided musical entertainment.**

Following her performance, Kate quite casually suggested that it would be interesting to see the American Flag projected onto the "Stage Curtains".

This novel idea was intriguing to Dill who promptly installed a projector for the image, and a record player for sound. Experimenting, he and Bob Hudson worked out a combination light-and-sound presentation which the touring public heartily applauded. Impressive and emotionally stirring, the showing of the "Stage Curtains"with its remarkable lighting sequence, is accompanied by a recording of the Missouri Waltz. The American Flag is then projected onto the "Stage Curtains"to the accompanyment of a record-

"THE ADVENTURES OF TOM SAWYER"
Johnnie Whitaker takes a break with Bob Hudson and Lester Dill
during a recent filming of "The adventures of Tom Sawyer", in
which Johnnie played the starring role.(Courtesy-Meramec Caverns)

GOSPEL SINGING FESTIVAL
(Courtesy-Meramec Caverns)

ing of God Bless America sung by Kate Smith.

Many celebrities have walked the rocky corridors of Meramec Caverns besides Kate Smith. Among them have been Rory Calhoun, Charles Laughton, the Ames Brothers and Pearl Bailey. Even a four-legged actor, Lassie.

Pearl Bailey's publicized visit came in 1968 when she and an all black cast were appearing at the St. Louis Municipal Opera in a production of "Hello Dolly". Although Miss Bailey was an invited guest at the cave, it was not her first visit. She admitted to having been there many times before because she just happens to like caves.+

In 1966 an episode of the Lassie Television Show was filmed at the caverns. This particular feature concerned "the plight of two runaway boys (played by teenage actors Kevin Brodie and Donald Losby) who seek refuge in the caverns after the raft they're floating on down the Mississippi River breaks up.

"While wandering through the maze of tunnels, the boys are confronted by a 7-foot 2-inch giant portrayed by Hollywood actor Richard Kiel, who leads them to

safety above ground and a meeting with their distraught parents."++

The presence of the filming crew, along with the real live Lassie, was a sensational news getter.

More recently, a new filming of "The Adventures of Tom Sawyer" by Mark Twain, was done, using Meramec Caverns for some of the underground scenes.⊕

The reason film producers take such a likeing to Meramec Caverns is because of the physical layout of the cave passages, their large size (camera crews, equipment and filming require a great amount of space), and the electrical power available. The cave has two electrical systems--one to supply power for guided tours; and a second to provide power for use in the "Ballroom". The second system is fed by a 7,200 volt cable and requires a 1,000 pound transformer. During the filming of a cave documentary several years ago, a camera crew utilized 45,000 watts of electricity to illuminate just one room of the cave.

More recently, Gospel Singing Festivals have become a Fall tradition at the cave. The first such festival, held in the late 1960's, featured eight of the nation's top television Gospel Singing groups (such as the Blackwood Brothers, the Stamps Quartet, etc.) So great was the attraction, the cave's "Ballroom" chamber was unable to accommodate the crowd. More than 3,000 people packed the underground auditorium and thousands were turned away for lack of room. Later festivals have spotlighted fewer all-time favorites to reduce the crowd to a manageable size.¢¢

★   ★   ★

The success of Meramec Caverns is, in a sense, a measure of the skills and genius of Lester B. Dill, although the hard work of his family, friends and employees has contributed substantially. Yet it has been the devotion and steadfast loyalty of Bob Hudson which has best sustained the enterprise.

Bob Hudson, the St. Louis boy was was "bowled over" at the age of thirteen by the magnificence of Meramec Caverns. He hired on in 1936 at 50¢ a-day plus food and lodging, which were Depression Day wages.

Young though he was, Bob had "a feeling" for the cave which quickly became apparent to his superiors. "I soon doubled his wages," Dill says. "He was worth every penny of it."

Bob began by tying bumper strips on cars, cleaning lanterns, scrubbing rest-rooms, and selling soft drinks down by La Jolla Spring where the Concession Stand was located.

To be a guide was his first ambition. Dill and Peterson sensed the potential "caveman" in this energetic city boy they had taken on. They were hardly surprised to discover him to be "a natural" at guiding.

The advent of U.S. involvement in WWII and Bob's 18th birthday coincided. He saw action overseas, and, with the wars end, returned to become a full-time employee at Meramec Caverns. Even then he knew something few young men know at such an early age--where he wanted to go in life. He was determined to make "cave work" his career.

Thirty-two years have come and gone since Bob made that decision. They have not always been easy years but they have been rewarding in terms of life satisfaction. As Bob said once "What you see here at Meramec Caverns is the story of my life."

From the position of parking lot attendant and bumper strip boy, he has worked his way up to Manager of Meramec Caverns. Says Les Dill "Bob Hudson deserves a lot of the credit for the success of my cave. I couldn't have done it without him."

Bob Hudson stands beside historic marker at Meramec Caverns, 1977. (Photo by Johnson)

119

TODAY'S "BALLROOM"
The beautiful "Ballroom" as it appears today, prepared for a banquet.
(Courtesy-Meramec Caverns)

Bob's wife Betty, and his three daughters, Bette, Judy and Robin, have all worked at the caverns for periods of time through the years.

Les Dill's fertile imagination has envisioned many ideas for the development and promotion of Meramec Caverns. But an idea, once born, must be executed with precision and skill if it is to succeed. The implementation of most of Dill's bold plans for the past two decades has been the sole responsibility of one remarkable publicity engineer--Bob Hudson. The results speak for themselves.

Bob Hudson, along with Les Dill, is largely responsible for the founding of the Missouri Caves Association (MCA), a non-profit organization of Missouri cave owners and operators devoted to the conservation and development of Missouri caves. Bob has served the MCA in many capacities from Secretary to President.

But Bob has been more than just a cave promoter concerned with ticket sales, the creation of interesting displays, guide training, advertising and public relations work.

"When the Rural Electric Association (REA) first came in years ago," says Les Dill "a lot of people were afraid to work with wires and electricity. But even before REA we installed a power generator for lighting at Meramec Caverns. Bob was here when we did that and familiarized himself with wiring."

That was the beginning of Bob's training as an "underground electrician, artist and technician." With each decade he became more and more involved in the craft of "cave lighting" until he had mastered its peculiar and demanding needs. Gifted with an intuitive "touch" for design, and an "eye for beauty" he became a master at the craft. The presentation of Meramec Caverns in word, sound and lighting has become a masterpiece of the show cave world. More recently, Bob has directed the lighting of two additional caves--Onondaga and Missouri Caverns. Both caves, former competitors of Meramec Caverns, are now owned by Les Dill.

Les Dill, undoubtedly the world's most widely known, respected and emulated caveman, was one of the first Missourians to widely promote Missouri as a "vacation state". He was one of the first to use bumper stickers as a means of advertising; one of the first to use radio for advertizing a natural cave as an attraction. He is the man who coined the expression "Missouri--The Cave State"; the man who initiated legislative action in the 1940's to establish a "cave inspection" law for Missouri--a model other states have envied. Since 1947 all Missouri caves open to the public have been subject to an annual inspection by the Missouri Department of Labor Standards to insure public safety.

Les Dill, the "sleepy-eyed rustic" from the Missouri hills who has devoted his life to selling Missouri caves as wholesome family entertainment just as persistently as he has sold Missouri to the nation about him.

This man, whose stubborness is matched only by his "dogged determination" and perserverance to succeed where others have failed, is a Missouri farm boy that must not be judged solely on the visible quality of his material possessions.

Lester B. Dill has a love for caves, for nature, for his fellow man that often transcends his drive to accumulate. For decades he has quietly supported innumerable humanitarian activities and cave research projects without remuneration. He was one of the first Missourians to join the National Speleological Society. And he has given both a financial and psychological support to scores of individuals interested in the study of caves.

And, in more recent years, he has, at great personal expense, fought bureau-

cratic encroachment upon Missouri's irreplacable and endangered natural wonders. His efforts to conserve and preserve the best Missouri has to offer as an everlasting heritage for generations of Missourians yet to be born, is an untold story and has been an environmental Godsend to the State of Missouri.

Les Dill, the man who helped organize the Missouri Caves Association and the National Caves Association, has always maintained a superb sense of history and an exact understanding of the role he wishes to have in it.

It would be easy to find fault with this man whose temperament is so ambivalent. He has a passion for life, a drive for success, and a shrewdness of intellect that defies most of us.

He can be overwhelming in his convictions and demanding nature. Yet, his baffling genius remains undiminished. He has been an inspiration to decades of cave owners and operators. He has been America's Number One Caveman for nearly 40 years. It is not likely that any of us will live to see his records of achievement in the show cave industry ever surpassed. That is the way it should be!

CIVIL DEFENSE PREPARATIONS
Civil Defense supplies being stored at Meramec Caverns. Lester B. Dill talks with Civil Defense Officials, left. Bob Hudson, center, directs Meramec Caverns employees. (Courtesy-Meramec)

Entrance to Meramec Caverns as it appears today.
(Courtesy-Meramec Caverns)

BIBLIOGRAPHY AND NOTES

INTRODUCTION

Page 5

* Nat. Caves Assn. proceedings,Oct. 1975. According to Tom Gibson, 1975 NCA Legislative Chairman, there were 167 operating show caves in the U.S. in 1975; See also Nat. Speleological Society *News*, May 1976.

** The American Spelean History Assn. was established in 1967.

+ Listed as Salt Peter Cave and/or Saltpeter Cave in several 19th Century publications.

Page 6

◊ *Dictionary of Humorous Quotations* Evan Esar, 1964.

++ *Franklin County Tribune*, Oct. 5, 1966, "America's Number One Cave Man Is A Franklin County Resident" by Ann Watson

◊◊ *St. Louis Globe Democrat*, Aug. 9, 1959, "A Back Country Barnum Packs Hole In Ground" by Beulah Schacht. Probably the first to make this comparison; see also *Depths of the Earth* by Wm. R. Halliday, M.D., Harper & Row, Pub. 1966.

‡ *Houdini, The Man Who Walked Through Walls* by Wm. L. Gresham, Manor Books Inc. 1975.

‡‡ Comparisons in this introduction based on biographical material presented in *The Fabulous Showman--The Life and Times of P.T. Barnum* by Irving Wallace, 1959.

⧧ *St. Louis Globe Democrat*, Aug.31, 1947 and Aug. 9, 1959; *St. Louis Post-Dispatch*, July 18, 1976.

⧧⧧ *Midwest Motorist*, Sept. 1968

PART I
THE FIRST 200 YEARS

LEGENDS OF GOLD

Page 11

* *A View of the Lead Mines of Missouri* by Henry R. Schoolcraft, N.Y.,Charles Wiley and Co.,1819.

** Ibid.

+ Ibid.

++ Ibid.

Page 12

* *History of Missouri*, Vol.I by Louis Houck, Chicago, R.R. Donnelley and Sons & Co., 1908.

+ Ibid.

** Ibid.

++ *Roads and Their Builders*, Prepared and designed by W. R. Nunn, Pub. by the Mo. State Hwy. Dept., no date.

◊ *Missouri, The Center State* by Walter B. Stevens, 1915; Controversy surrounds the travels of De Soto and researchers on both sides are considerably biased. Some maintain that De Soto and/ or his men penetrated far into the Missouri territories, others that he didn't. No adequate resolution of this debate is likely.

◊◊ *Missouri Magazine*, Oct. 1928, "Ancient Lore of Meramec State Park" by Wm. R. Draper.

‡ *Missouri Historical Review*, Vol. II, Oct. 1907-July 1908, "Rivers of Jefferson County from Old Landmarks Committee--Report To The Old Settlers Society, Sept. 15, 1906" by John L. Thomas.

Page 14

** Ibid.

* *Missouri and Missourians*, Vol. 1 by Shoemaker, 1943.

SALTPETRE, THE CAVERNS GIFT

Page 17

* Wm. Clark Breckenridge,"Early Gunpowder Making in Missouri", *Mo. Historical Review*,Oct.1925-July 1926, Vol. 20.

Page 18

* See Page 17, Reference *

** *Goodspeed's History of Franklin, Jefferson, Washington, Crawford and Gasconade Counties, Missouri*, Goodspeed Pub. Co., Chicago, 1888.

+ See Reference * above.

++ See Reference ** above.

◊ *Missouri Magazine*, Feb. 1935, "Stone Age Men of Crawford County" by Carl H. Chapman. He also states "Nearly every cave that was large enough and was not too wet, was used either for a short time or permanently by the Indian or his predecessors.";See also *A Century Passes But Memory Lingers On, The Centennial History of Sullivan, Missouri*.

‡ See Page 11, Reference * ; See also *Frontier Iron, The Meramec Iron Works 1826-1876* by James D. Norris, Worzalla Pub. Co., Stevens Points,Wisc. 1964.

‡‡ *A Century Passes But Memory Lingers On, The Centennial History of Sullivan, Mo.*

◊◊ *The Story of Old Ste. Genevieve* by Gregory M. Granzwa, Patrice Press, Inc. 1967.

Page 19

* *Historic Missouri, A Pictorial Narrative of our State*, State Historical Society of Mo. 1959; See also *Roads and Their Builders*, Mo. State Hwy. Commission.

** *Missouri Historical Review*, State Historical Soc. of Mo. Vol. 24.

Page 20

◊ *Saltpeter Caves And Virginia History* by Burton Faust, 1964: Faust, an authority on saltpetre mining, has written extensively on the subject. Methods of identification can also be found in his saltpetre manuscripts relative to Mammoth Cave in Kentucky.

* See Page 5, Reference *

Page 21

◊ Based on studies by Burton Faust.

+ See Page 5, Reference *

Page 22

++ Meramec Caverns commercial brochure, 1975.

◊ *Spanish Land Claims In Missouri* by Eugene M. Violette, 1921; *Franklin County Atlas, 1898*.

SETTLERS, SALTPETRE AND SURVIVAL

Page 23

* *A History of Missouri* by Jonas Viles, 1944.

** *Onondaga, The Mammoth Cave of Missouri* by H. Dwight Weaver, Discovery Enterprises, 1973.

+ Ibid.

++ See Page 12, Reference ++

◊ *Sesqui-Centennial Edition, Historical Review of Franklin Co., Missouri 1818-1968* by Melvin Roblee and Vera L. Osiek. Moore Enterprises Inc., Printers.

◊◊ "Stephen and Dorcas Sullivan Monument", a historical sketch by S. H. Sullivan, Sr. From a newspaper clipping circa 1913 owned by John Sullivan.

Page 24

* See Page 23, Reference ◊

** Based on the research of Burton Faust concerning saltpetre mining in the Appalachian region.

+ See Page 23, Reference ◊

++ See Page 23, Reference ◊

Page 26

◊ See Page 23, Reference ◊; There were a number of Maupins who settled in the county early in the 1800's. Most were young and had slaves, however, Col. Ernest Maupin was the exception and best known of the Maupins. Although he was a southerner and a slave holder when the war began, he went into war in 1861 and fought with the Union, believing the unity of the nation was worth more than slavery. See *Atlas of Franklin Co.,Mo., 1878.*

◊◊ See Page 23, Reference ◊

‡ Breckenridge quote: *The Missouri Gazette and Illinois Advertiser* St. Louis, Oct. 14, 1814 and Nov. 30, 1816.

+ See Page 18, Reference **

++ *Missouri Historical Review*, Mo. Historical Soc., Vol. 24,p.608

* See Page 18, Reference **; Additional information on saltpetre mining and gunpowder making can be found in *The Journal of Spelean History*, American Spelean History Assn., Vol. 4, No.1,January-March 1971, "Early Gunpowder Making and Saltpetre Mining In Missouri" by H.Dwight Weaver.

CAVES AND CANNON THUNDER

Page 28

* *History of Miller Co.*, Vol.I by Clyde Jenkins.

** Ibid.

+ *Ozark Speleograph*, Lake Ozark Grotto(NSS),Vol.5,No.1,Jan.1975 "Outlaw Years In The Osage River Basin" by H.Dwight Weaver

Page 29

* Meramec Caverns commercial brochure.

** See Page 18, Reference **

Page 30

* See Page 18, Reference ‡‡

** *Chicago Daily Tribune*, Jan. 21, 1954, "By The Way" with Thomas Morrow.

Page 31

+ See Page 23, Reference ◊◊

‡ See Page 18, Reference ‡‡

* Meramec Caverns commercial brochure.

‡‡ See Page 20, Reference ◊

THE LEGENDARY JESSE JAMES

Page 33

* *Jesse James The Outlaw* by Henry J. Walker, 1961.

** Lester B. Dill, in conversation with the author, 1975.

Page 35

* See Page 33, Reference **

** For additional information on the Jesse James legend see Meramec Caverns commercial brochure; also *The Truth About Jesse James* by Phyllis Argall, 1955;also *St. Louis Globe Democrat*, July 11, 1943 "Five Story Cavern Ready For Wartime Tourists"; also *Medallic Monthly* Vol. 1, No. 2, Nov. 1967,Mandeville, La. "Reward--$10,000 -- Reward: A Little-Known Story About Jesse James"; also *New Haven Conn. Register*, April 23, 1961 "Dill Pioneered, Carved Niche For Himself As A Cave Promoter"

THE RAILROAD AND RICHES

Page 37

* *Government Tract Book*, Franklin County, Union, Mo.

Page 38

+ See Page 23, Reference ◊◊

++ *Campbells Gazateer of Missouri*, St. Louis, 1874.

◊ Ida Schmuke, Stanton, Mo., interview July 14, 1975.

◊◊ Lester B. Dill, in conversation with the author, 1975.

‡ Franklin County Records, *W. D. Book 11*, p. 402.

‡‡ Franklin County Records, *W. D. Books 11* (1872), 12 (1875) 14 (1879), 17(1879), 20 (1884), 28 (1887), 35(1891), and 44 (1895)

‡ *The Centennial Biographical Directory of Franklin Co., Mo.* by Herman Gottlieb Kiel, 1925.

Page 39

‡‡ Franklin County Records, *E. D. 121*, p. 538, *Abstract Deed Index* No. 22, 1930-48; Also *Misc. Record Bk. 118*, p. 264.

DANCES AND DISCOVERY

Page 41

* Plat of the Town of Stanton, 1898, *Franklin County Atlas*.

** *Missouri State Gazateer and Business Directory* by R.L. Polk and Co., St. Louis, 1893-94.

+ Ibid.

++ Ida Schmuke, Stanton, Mo., interview, July 14, 1975.

ɸ Eddie Door, Virden, Illinois, interview, Feb. 1976.

ɸɸ Ibid.

Page 42

* Handbill, 1895, property of Lester B. Dill.

** *Sullivan Sentinel*, Friday, July 26, 1901; Feb. 14, 1902.

Page 43

+ Ida Schmuke, Stanton, Mo., interview July 14, 1975.

++ See Page 41, Reference ɸ

Page 44

* Lester B. Dill, in conversation with author May 25, 1975; also Ida Schmuke, interview, 1975.

ɸ *Sullivan Sentinel*, July 1901.

ɸɸ *Sullivan Sentinel*, May 1902

‡ *Sullivan Sentinel*, July 3, 1903

‡‡ *Sullivan Sentinel*, Oct. 1905.

‖ *Missouri Historical Review*, Mo. Historical Society.

Page 45

* *Sullivan Sentinel*, June 1906.

** John Sullivan, Sullivan, Mo. in conversation with the author in 1975.

+ *Sullivan Sentinel*, July 26,1901

Page 47

+ *Sullivan Sentinel*, Aug.16,1901.

PART II
A MAN CALLED DILL

SAVED BY SMOKE
Page 52

* *Altoona Mirror*, Altoona, Pa. June 14, 1967, "Missouri Man Builds Empire Out of Caves".

** This story of Dill's adventure in Onyx Cave has been printed many times over the years. In a conversation with the author on July 13,1975, Les Dill said "that's a true story about getting lost and cigarette smoke helped us find the cave entrance."

+ Lester B. Dill, in conversation with author, July 13, 1975.

LESTER LEARNS AT FISHERS CAVE
Page 53

* Lester B. Dill, July 13, 1975.

Page 54

** Lester B. Dill, July 13, 1975.

+ *Missouri Speleology*, Vol.II,No. 2, April 1960.

++ *Atlas of Franklin County, Mo. 1878*.

ɸ *Goodspeed's History of Franklin, Jefferson, Washington, Crawford and Gasconade Counties, Missouri*, Goodspeed Pub. Co., Chicago, 1888.

ɸɸ *Franklin County Atlas, 1898*.

‡ *Sullivan News*, Feb. 17, 1927.

‡‡ Ibid.

‖ *Caves of Missouri* by J Harlen Bretz, Mo. Geo. Survey, 1956.

Page 55

‡‡ *Mo. Historical Review*, Vol. 24 p. 608, Mo. Hist. Soc.

* *A History of Missouri* by Jonas Viles, 1944.

** See Page 54, Reference ɸ

+ See Page 18, Reference ‡‡

++ See Page 23, Reference ɸ

ɸ Eddie Miller, Camdenton, Mo. interview Dec. 9, 1974.

‡ Lester B. Dill, 1975.

THE DILL-PICKLE PARK

Page 57

* *St. Louis Globe-Democrat*, Aug. 31, 1947, "Les Dill and Partner Have Made Mint Of Old Mine".

** See Page 18, Reference ‡‡

+ Ibid.

++ *Sullivan News*, Jan. 1926

ɸ *Sullivan News*, July 1926

Page 58

ɸɸ *Sullivan News*, July 1926

‡ *Sullivan News*, Feb. 17, 1927 "Naming The Park"; see also *Sullivan News*, Feb. 24, 1927 "Naming The Park" and *Sullivan News*, March 3, 1927.

‡‡ *Sullivan News*, March 10, 1927

‖ *Sullivan News*, Aug. 1927

* *Sullivan News*, Feb. 2, 1928

Page 59

** *St. Louis Globe-Democrat*, Sept. 9, 1928, "Thousands Witness Dedication of New Meramec State Park"; *St. Louis Globe-Democrat* Sept. 2, 1928, "New Meramec Park at Sullivan To Be Dedicated Saturday. All Day Program Announced By The St. Louis Chamber of Commerce."

SQUARE NAILS AND TALL TALES

Page 61

* Lester B. Dill interview, 1976

** Ibid. Les Dill used similar words to describe this period in an article titled "How I Made A Million" published in a mens' magazine in the 1950's.

Page 62

ɸ Eddie Miller, Camdenton, Mo. interview Dec. 9, 1974.

ɸɸ Ibid.

Page 63

‡ *The Midwest Motorist*, Sept.1968 "Tall Tales and Square Nails"by Dickson Terry.

‡‡ See Page 62, Reference ɸ

‖ *Sullivan News*, Dec. 6, 1928

‖‖ *Sullivan News*, Oct. 16, 1930.

* *Sullivan News*, June 12, 1930.

** *Sullivan News*, Aug. 6, 1931.

+ Ibid.

Page 64

++ *Sullivan News*, Aug. 4, 1932.

ɸ *Missouri Magazine*, March 1950, "Meramec Park--Missouri's Caveland" by Townsend Godsey.

ɸɸ *Sullivan News*, June 18, 1931.

‡ *Sullivan News*, July 9, 1931.

Page 65

‡ *Sullivan News*, June 1, 1933.

CHARLEY AND LES

Page 67

* Lester B. Dill, 1976.

** *Onondaga, The Mammoth Cave of Missouri*, by H. Dwight Weaver 1973.

+ Lester B. Dill, 1976.

Page 68

++ Bob Shatz, Stanton, Mo., interview 1976.

ɸ Ibid.

ɸɸ Mary Dill, Stanton, Mo.,interview, Feb. 1976.

Page 69

‡ See Page 68, Reference ++

‡‡ *Centennial Biographical Directory of Franklin County, 1925*.

‖ See Page 68, Reference ++

‖‖ See Page 68, Reference ++

* Maude Woodcock,Sullivan,Mo.1976

** See Page 68, Reference ++

+ "How I Made A Million" by Les Dill, See Page 61, Ref. **

Page 70

++ Franklin Co. Records, Union,Mo. 1933.

ɸ Lester B. Dill, 1976

ɸɸ Ibid.

‡ See Page 68, Reference ++

‡‡ See Page 70, Reference ++

‖ Lester B. Dill, 1976.

Page 71

‡‡ See Page 68, Reference ++

* Ibid.

** Betty Pruett, Stanton, Mo., in-
    terview 1976.

Page 72

+ Lester B. Dill, 1976.

++ Ibid.

⊕ *Sullivan News*, July 6, 1976.

LES AND PETE

Page 75

* Eddie Miller, Camdenton,Mo.,in-
   terview Dec. 9, 1974.

+ *St. Louis Globe-Democrat*, Aug.
   31, 1947 "Les Dill and Partner
   Have Made Mint Of Old Mine."

** Lester B. Dill, 1976.

++ See Reference + above.

Page 76

⊕ Eddie Door, Virden, Ill., interview, 1976.

⊕⊕ Lester B. Dill, 1976.

‡ Mary Dill, Stanton, Mo. 1976.

Page 77

‡‡ See Page 75, Reference +

‡ *St. Louis Post-Dispatch*, July
   18, 1976, "Fanfare Of A Cave
   Man" by Robert Sanford.

‡‡ See Page 75, Reference +

* Mary Dill, Stanton,Mo. 1976.

Page 78

** Eddie Door interview, 1976.

+ Eddie Miller interview, 1974.

++ Lester B. Dill, 1975.

⊕ See Page 77, Reference ‡

Page 79

⊕⊕ *Midwest Motorist*, Sept. 1968.

‡ *Independence Missouri Examiner*,
   Independence Mo., March 1961
   "Dill Puts Money In Caves But
   Gets More In Return" by Fred
   Baum.

‡‡ Eddie Door, interview, 1976.

‡‡ Lester B. Dill, 1976.

JESSE'S SECRET

Page 81

* Betty Pruett, interview, 1976.

** Ibid.

Page 82

+ Unidentified news Clipping,
   summer of 1961.

++ Ibid.

⊕ *Ravensw'd News*, Chicago, Aug.
   5, 1941.

Page 83

⊕⊕ *Chicago Daily News*, July 12,1941

‡ Unidentified, undated news clipping, believed local. "Radio
   Gives Good Reception In Cave"

Page 84

‡‡ *Watchman Advocate*,St. Louis,Mo.
   July 1941.

‡ Lester B. Dill, 1975.

Page 85

‡ *Caves of Missouri* by J Harlen
   Bretz, Mo. Geo. Survey, 1956.

THE ARMY AND THE GUIDES

Page 87

* Eddie Miller, interview, 1974.

** Bob Hudson, interview, 1976.

+ *Watchman Advocate*,St. Louis,Mo.
   Nov. 7. 1941.

Page 89

++ *Journal of Commerce*, Chicago,
   Ill., July 31,1941 "119th Field
   Artillery Took Sullivan By
   Storm"

⊕ Bob Hudson, interview, 1976.

⊕⊕ Ibid.

Page 90

‡ Bob Hudson, interview, 1976.

‡‡ Eddie Miller, interview,1974.

Page 91

‡ Bob Hudson, interview, 1976.

‡‡ Ibid.

* Eddie Miller,interview, 1974.

Page 92

** Eddie Door,interview, 1976.

+ Ibid.

Page 93

++ Lester B. Dill, 1976.

⊕ Ida Schmuke,interview, 1976.

⊕⊕ Eddie Door, interview, 1976.

‡ Eddie Miller, interview, 1974.

Page 94

‡ Bob Hudson, interview, 1976.

‡‡ Ibid.

JESSE'S LEGACY

Page 95

* *Caves of Missouri* by J Harlen
   Bretz, 1956.

Page 97

** *Caves of Missouri* by J Harlen
   Bretz, 1956.

+ *MMV Underground*, Vol. 2, No. 1
   April 1959.

Page 98

++ *Wellston Journal* (Ill.?) July
   22, 1942.

Page 99

⊕ See Page 98, Reference ++

Page 100

⊕⊕ *Berwyn Illinois Life*, July 25,
   1941.

BOMBS, BALLYHOO AND THE "A" CARD

Page 101

* *Monroe County Clarion*, Columbia
   Illinois, July 4, 1945.

Page 102

** Unidentified,undated news clipping, Lester B. Dill, owner.

Page 103

+ See Page 102, Reference **

++ See Page 75, Reference +

⊕ "Missourian Mines Dollars of
   Tourists at Elaborate Cave"
   Wilkes Barre, Pa., *Independent*
   April 23, 1961.

Page 104

⊕⊕ Willmark Service System, Inc.
   250 W. 57th Street, New York
   (in 1948): Surveys by "D.C.Z.
   Reports"

Page 106

‡ See Page 104, Reference ⊕⊕

THE RETURN OF JESSE JAMES

Page 107

* *Midwest Motorist*, Sept. 1968.

** *St. Louis Globe-Democrat*, St.
   Louis, Mo., Aug. 9, 1959.

Page 108

+ *St. Louis Post-Dispatch*, July
   18, 1976.

⊕ *Bulletin*, Brownwood, Texas
   "Jesse (J Frank Dalton) Says He
   Has $2 Million In Loot Near
   Fort Sill" Jan. 10, 1950; *New
   York Times*, New York "Jesse
   James Is Bed-Ridden But Still
   Powerful Actor" Jan. 10, 1950;
   Denver Post,Denver, Colo. "Loot
   Cited As Proof He's The Real
   James" Jan. 10, 1950.

Page 109

⊕⊕ *The Truth About Jesse James* by
   Phyllis Argall, 1953.

‡ *Reporter*, Sweetwater, Texas,
   "Jesse James, 102. Gets To New
   York With His Story" Jan. 10,
   1950.

Page 110

‡‡ *State Journal*, Lansing Mich.,
   Jan. 11, 1950.

‡ Ibid.

‡‡ *St. Louis Post-Dispatch*, See Page 108, Reference +

* *St. Louis Globe-Democrat*, Aug. 9, 1959.

A PARADE OF PROMOTIONS

Page 113

* *Daily Standard*, Excelsior Springs, Mo. June 24, 1969,"Tourists Dig Cave of Jesse James".

** *St. Louis Globe-Democrat*,Aug.9, 1959 "A Back Country Barnum Packs Hole In Ground."

+ *Beaumont Enterprise*, Beaumont, Texas, Sept. 1955.

Page 114

++ *Decatur Review*, Decatur, Ill. July 11, 1959 "Missouri Caves 'Gopher Holes'".

⊕ *Depths of the Earth* by Wm. R. Halliday.

⊕⊕ See Page 113, Reference **

‡ Ibid.

Page 115

‡‡ *News and Courier*, Charleston, South Carolina, April 8, 1961, "Visitor Shocks New York; He Actually Likes Subways"; *World Telegram and Sun*, New York, N. Y., April 7, 1961, "Visitor On Caveman's Holiday Circulates Through Subways".

Page 116

‡ Lester B. Dill, 1976.

‡‡ *Sikeston Standard*, Sikeston,Mo. Aug. 3,1962,"Nation's Only Singing Guide At Meramec Caverns, Missouri".

Page 117

* "The Story About A Singing Cave Man At Meramec Caverns At Stanton Who Is Heard Of In New York", newsclipping, undated, unidentified.

** Lester B. Dill, 1976.

+ *Sullivan Tri-County News*, Sullivan, Mo. "Pearl Bailey Visits Meramec Caverns" Aug. 15, 1968; *Franklin County Tribune*, Union Mo. "Pearl Bailey and Troup Visit Meramec Caverns" Aug. 7, 1968.

++ *Franklin County Tribune*, Nov.16 1966; *Sturgis Daily Journal*, Michigan, June 17, 1966; *Rural Electric Missourian*, July 1966.

⊕ *Rural Electric Missourian*, Nov. 1972.

⊕⊕ "Gateway To The West Gospel Sing Present At The Beautiful Meramec Caverns, Saturday, Nov. 1, 1969." This poster listed James Blackwood and the Blackwood Brothers Quartet; Hovie Lister and the Statesmen Quartet; J. D.Sumner and the Stamps Quartet; The Imperials; Jack Hess and the Music City Singers The Oak Ridge Boys; Gateway Boys and Donna; and the Lester Family--all gospel singing groups of television and radio fame.

(Photo by Johnson)